selections from

David Crowder*Band
Give Us Rest

or (a requiem mass in c [the happiest of all keys])

ISBN 978-1-4584-2206-4

HAL•LEONARD®
CORPORATION

7777 W. BLUEMOUND RD. P.O. BOX 13819 MILWAUKEE, WI 53213

Visit Hal Leonard Online at
www.halleonard.com

OH GREAT GOD, GIVE US REST

Words and Music by DAVID CROWDER
and MATT MAHER

Quietly, with reflection

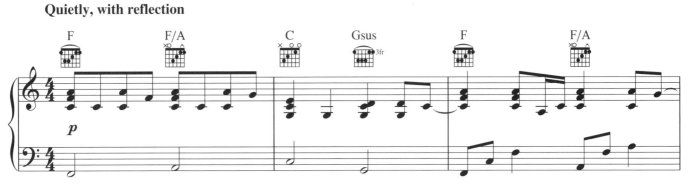

Oh great God, give us _____ rest. We're all worn thin from

all of this, the end of our hope with noth-ing left.

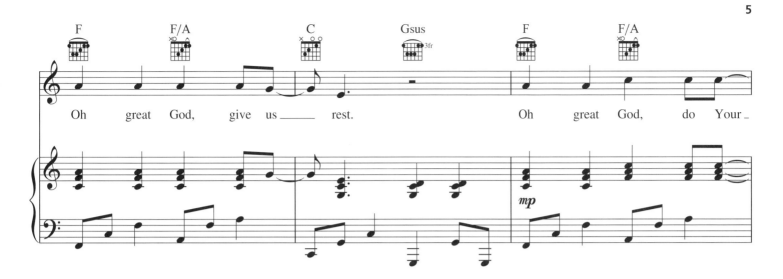

Oh great God, give us ____ rest. Oh great God, do Your ____

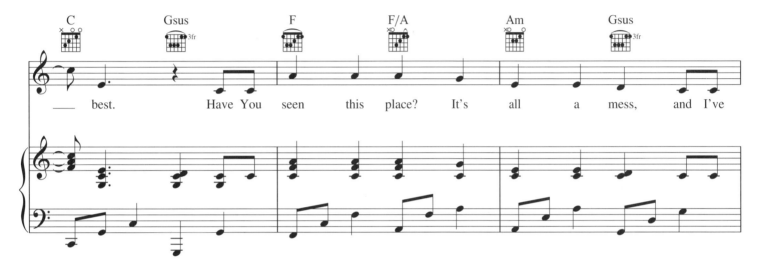

____ best. Have You seen this place? It's all a mess, and I've

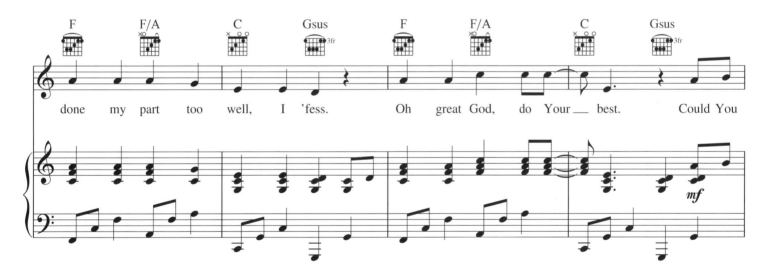

done my part too well, I 'fess. Oh great God, do Your ____ best. Could You

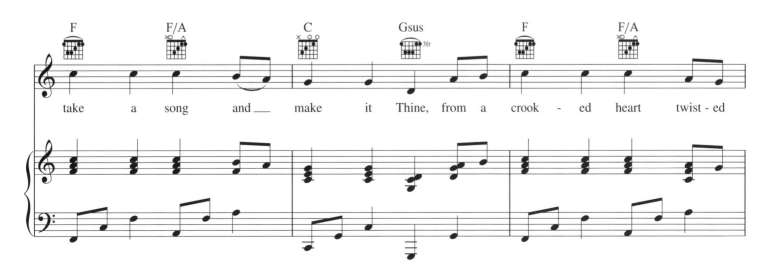

take a song and ____ make it Thine, from a crook - ed heart twist - ed

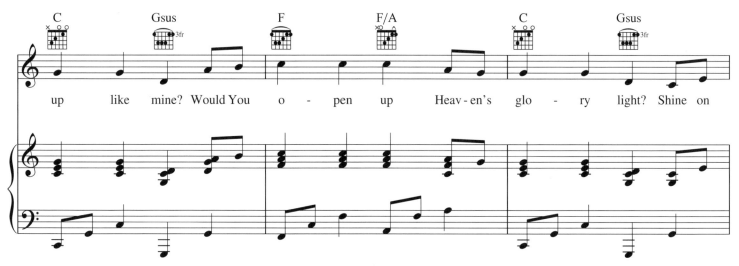

up like mine? Would You o - pen up Heav - en's glo - ry light? Shine on

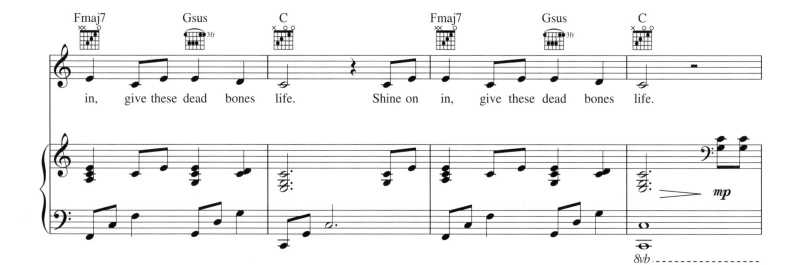

in, give these dead bones life. Shine on in, give these dead bones life.

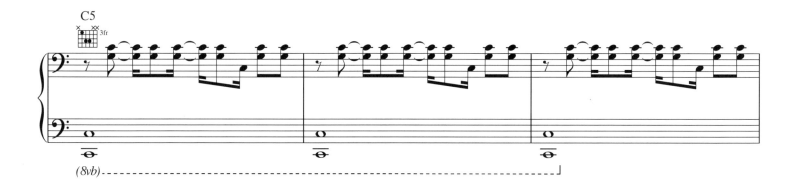

Let it shine, let it

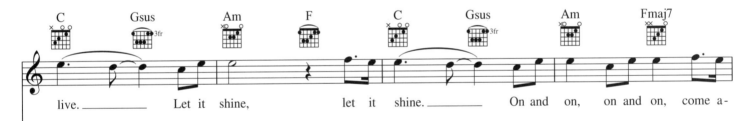

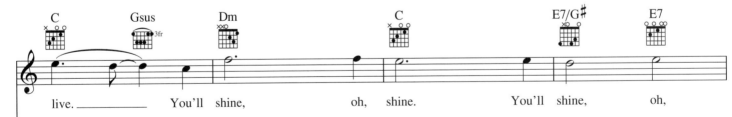

shine.   You'll shine,   oh, shine.   You'll shine,   oh, You'll

shine. _____

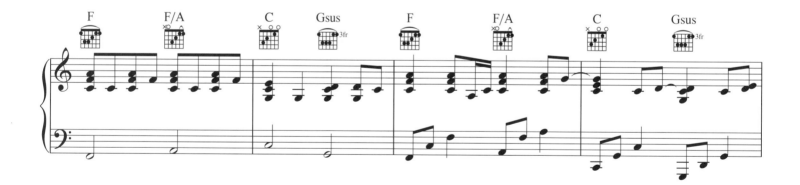

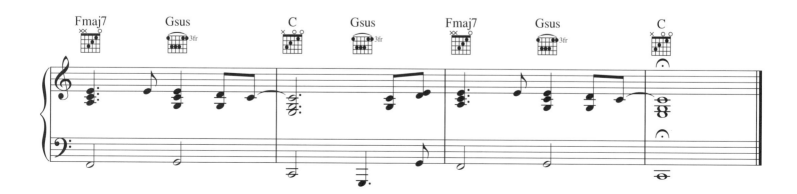

COME FIND ME

Words and Music by DAVID CROWDER,
JACK PARKER and JEREMY BUSH

With energy

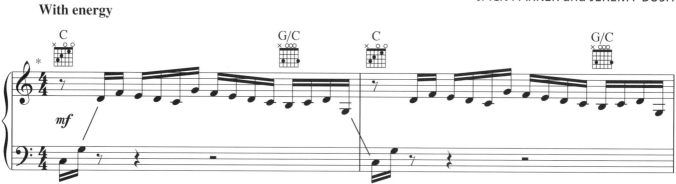

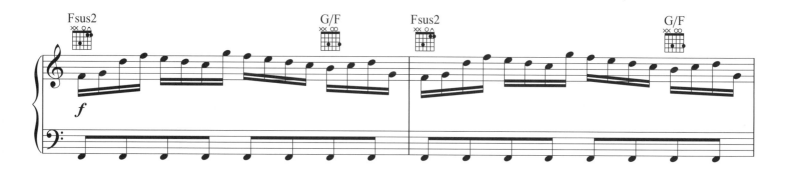

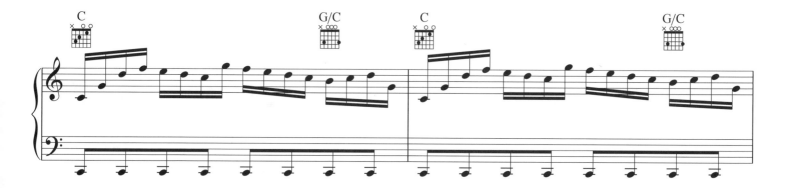

The One _

Recorded a half step higher.

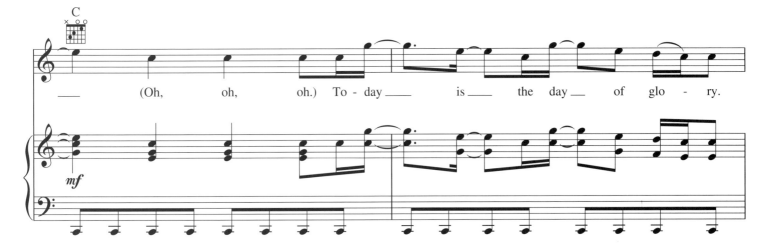

Oh day, what a day, ___ oh day, I'm Yours. Oh, day of

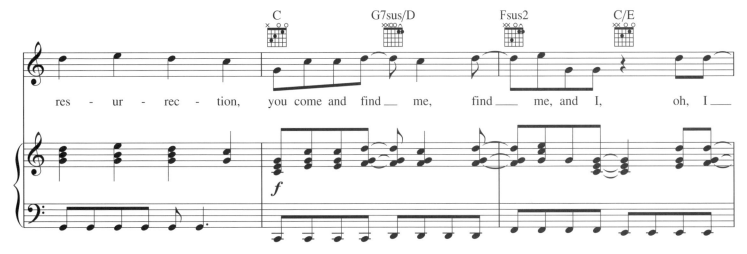

res - ur - rec - tion, you come and find ___ me, find ___ me, and I, oh, I ___

___ come a - live, ___ I ___ come a - live. ___ What can I do ___ but of -

To Coda

- fer my life? ___ Would-n't I ___ come a - live? ___ Oh, I'd ___ come a - live ___ a - gain.

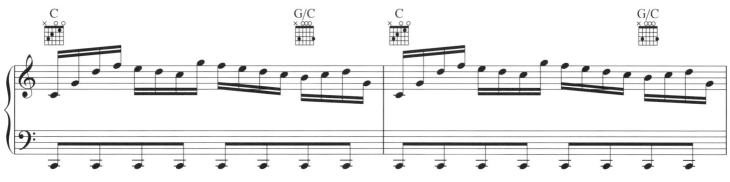

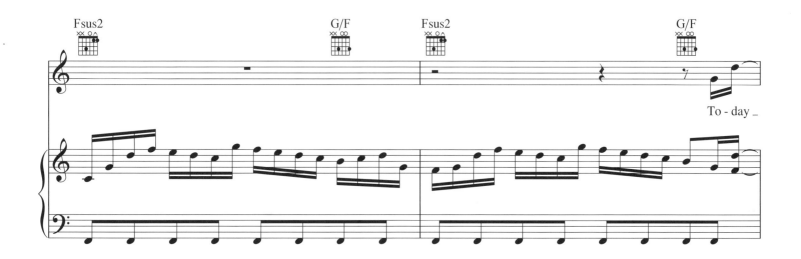

To - day

is the day I rise like the dawn, up out of death, oh, oh, oh,

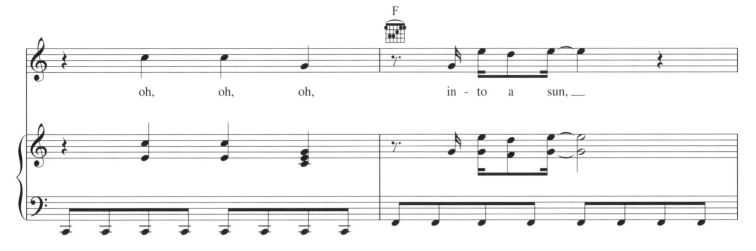

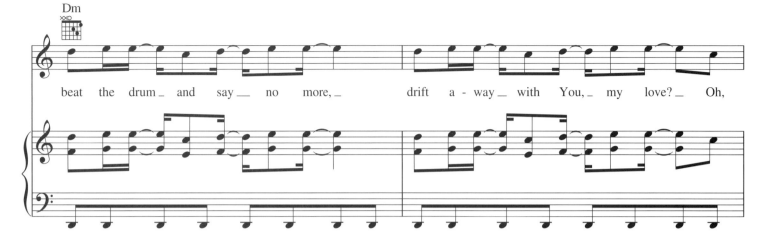

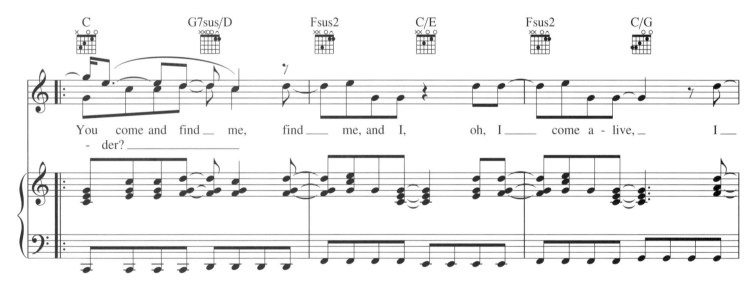

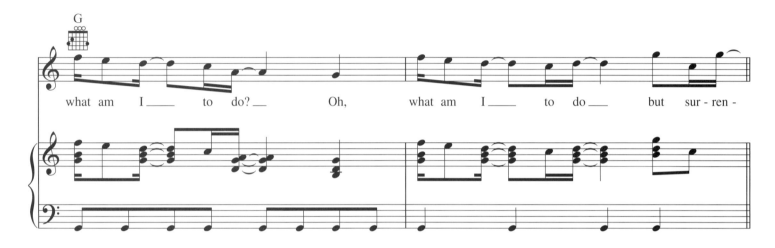

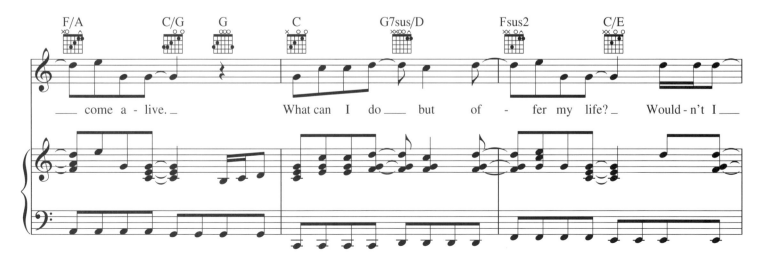

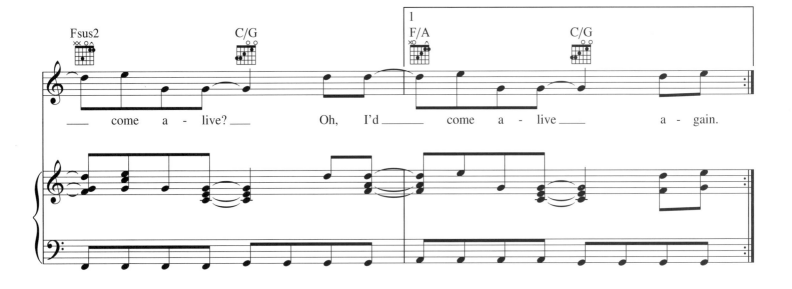

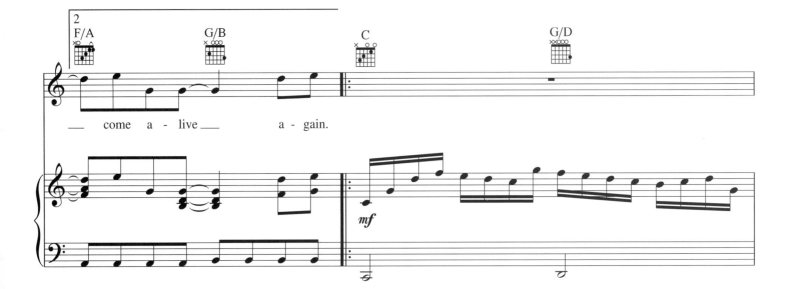

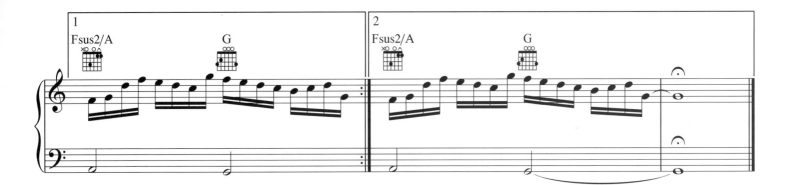

FALL ON YOUR KNEES

Words and Music by
DAVID CROWDER

Moderate Rock beat

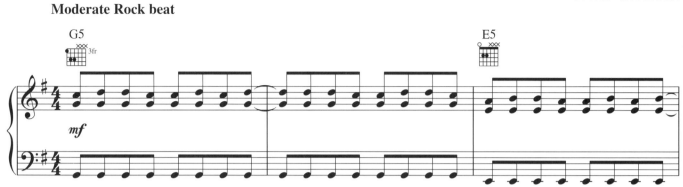

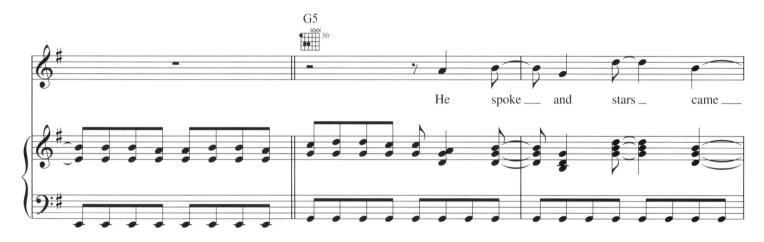

He spoke and stars came out.

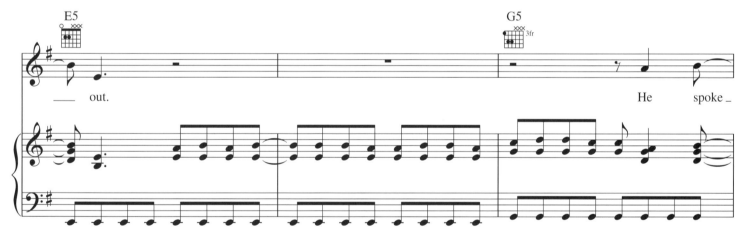

out. He spoke

and light-ning flashed, and thun-der broke the quiet.

He spoke, ___ and my heart, ___ it burst to life. ___

___ And all this

mys - ter - y di - vine. ___

Fall on your ___ knees, ___ for - giv - en and clean, ___ for - giv - en and free. ___

Oh, ___ my God, ___ oh, ___ my God, ___ it's too won-der-ful, ___

___ it's too won-der-ful. _____ A voice, ___

___ then all ___ of _____ this. A voice ___ that called __ me _____ "friend" in dark -

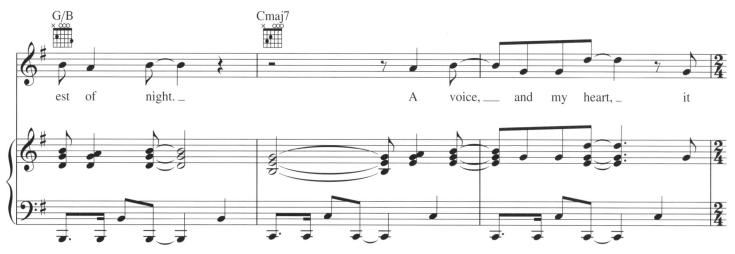

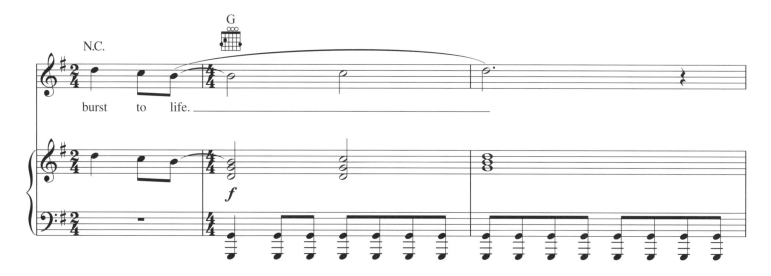

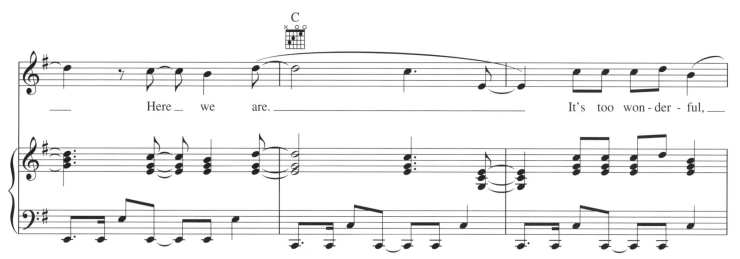

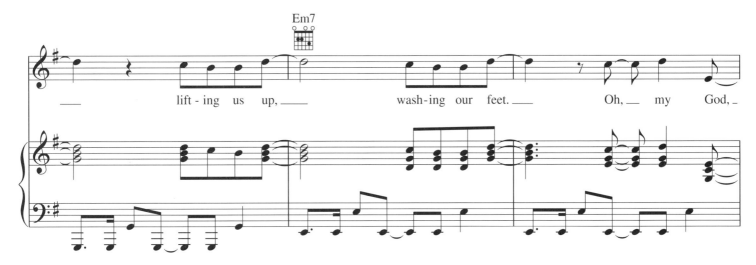

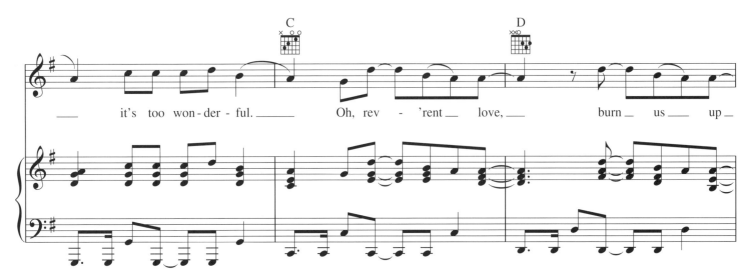

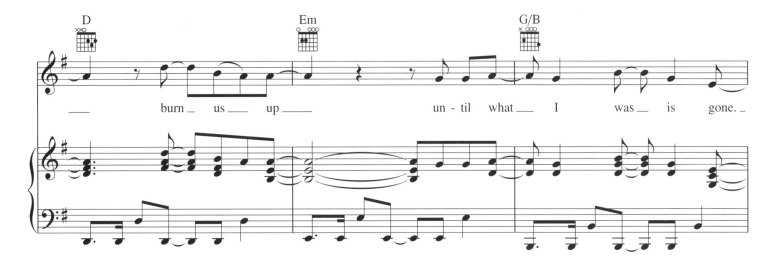

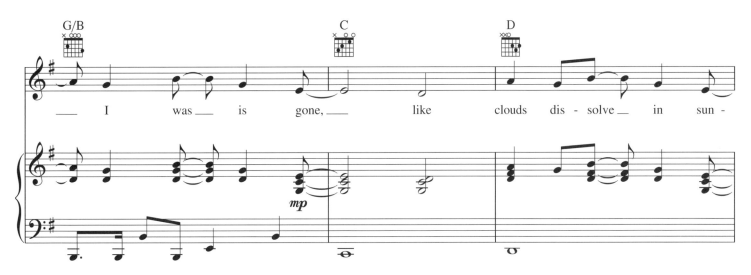

LET ME FEEL YOU SHINE

Words and Music by DAVID CROWDER
and MARK WALDROP

Moderate Rock beat

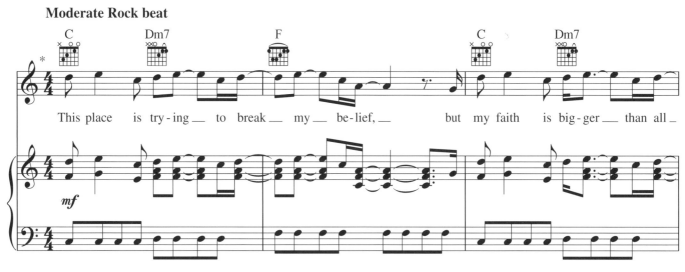

This place is try-ing __ to break __ my be-lief, __ but my faith is big-ger __ than all __

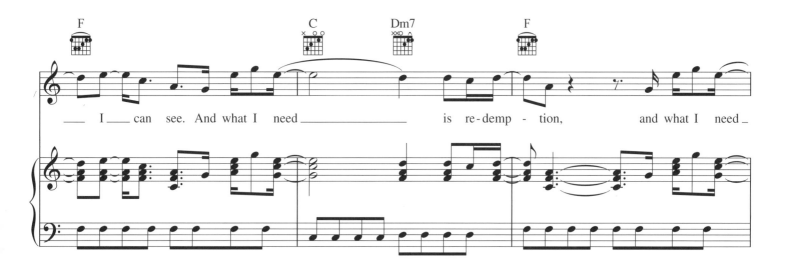

__ I __ can see. And what I need _____ is re-demp- tion, and what I need __

_____ is for You __ to put me back on my feet. Whoa, oh, oh. __

* *Recorded a half step lower.*

Whoa, oh,   oh, _

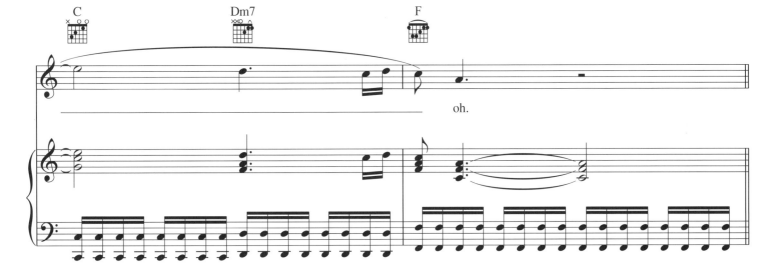

oh.

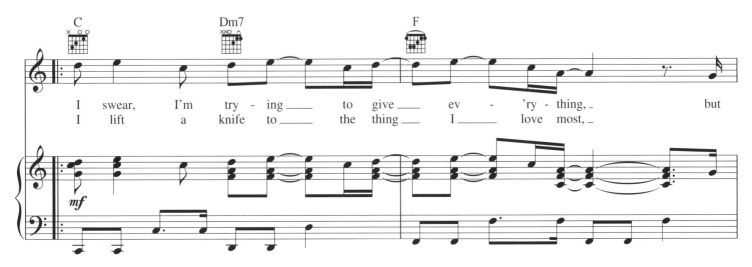

I swear, I'm try - ing _ to give _ ev - 'ry - thing, _   but

I lift a knife to _ the thing _ I _ love most, _

I fear I'm fall - ing; _ oh, make _ me _ be - lieve. _ And what I need _

pray - ing You'll come so _ that I _ can _ have both. _ And what I need _

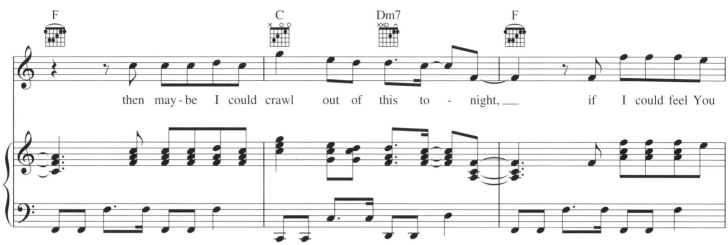

then may-be I could crawl out of this to-night, ___ if I could feel You

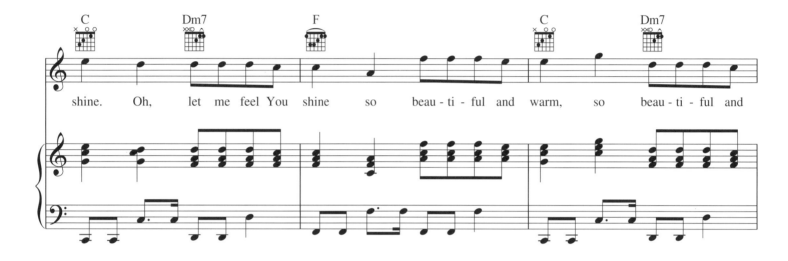

shine. Oh, let me feel You shine so beau-ti-ful and warm, so beau-ti-ful and

bright, like sun com-ing out of a rain - y sky. Oh, let me feel You

shine. Oh, let me feel You shine.   shine. Oh, let me feel You

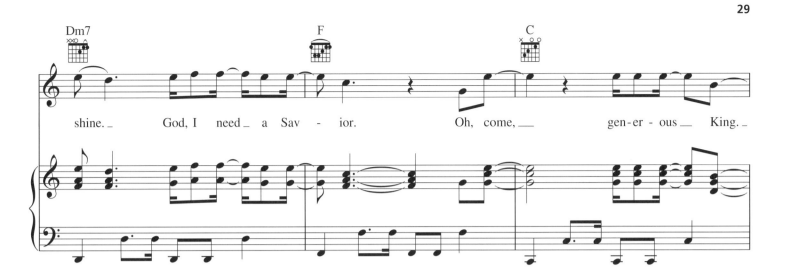

shine.__ God, I need__ a Sav - ior. Oh, come,__ gen-er-ous__ King.__

__ Oh, God, I need__ a Sav - ior to come__

__ res - cue__ me.__ Oh, let me feel You shine Your mag-nif-i-cent light.

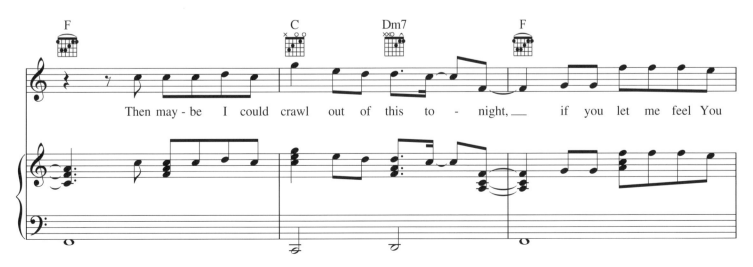

Then may-be I could crawl out of this to - night,__ if you let me feel You

BLESSEDNESS OF
EVERLASTING LIGHT

Words and Music by DAVID CROWDER
and MIKE HOGAN

Moderately fast Waltz

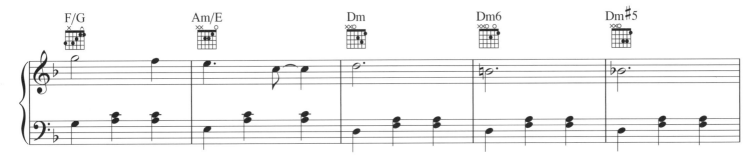

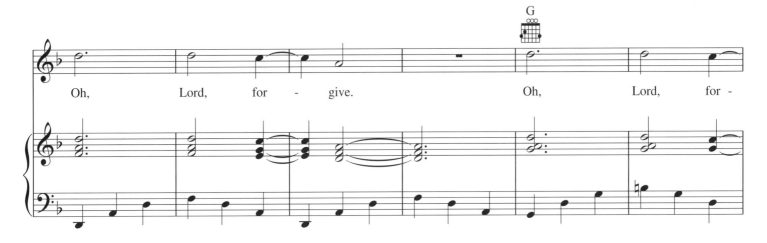

Oh, Lord, for - give. Oh, Lord, for -

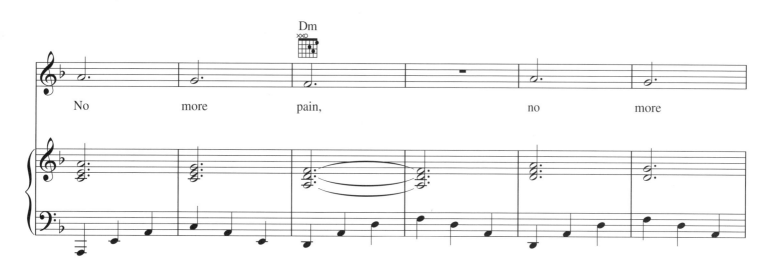

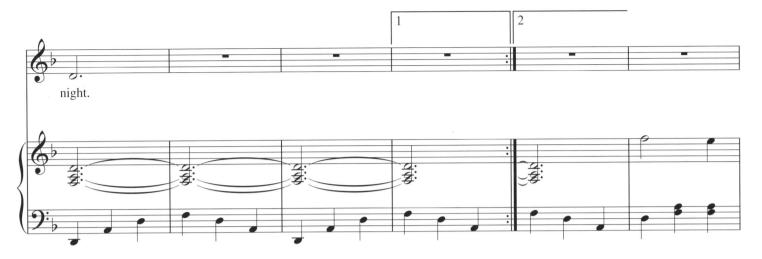

night.

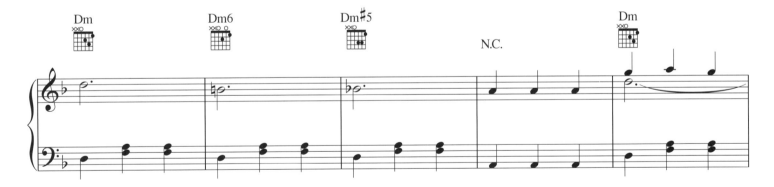

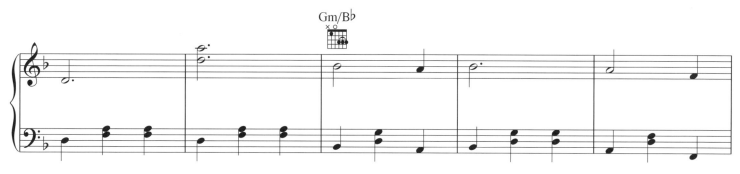

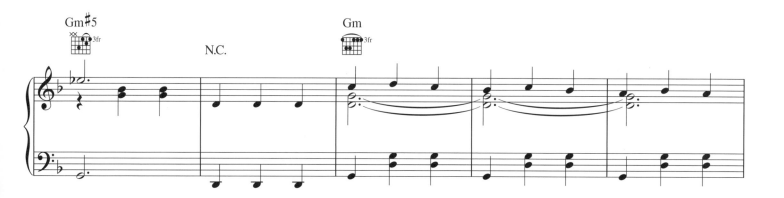

Bless - ed - ness of _____ ev -

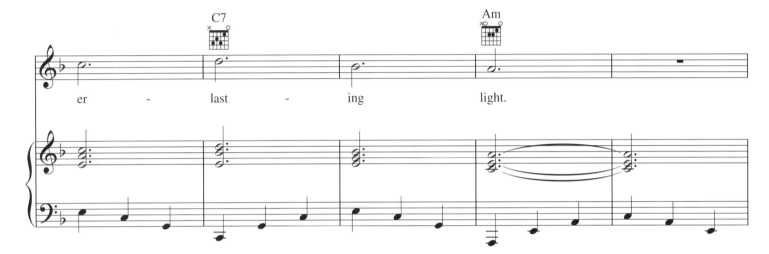

er - last - ing light.

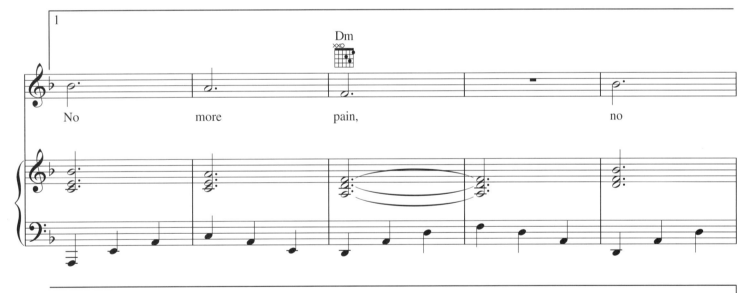

No more pain, no

more night. Oh.

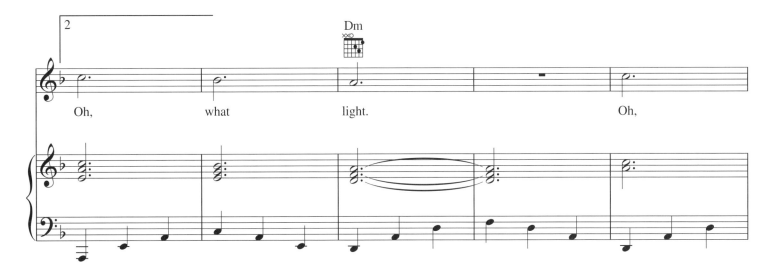

Oh,   what   light.   Oh,

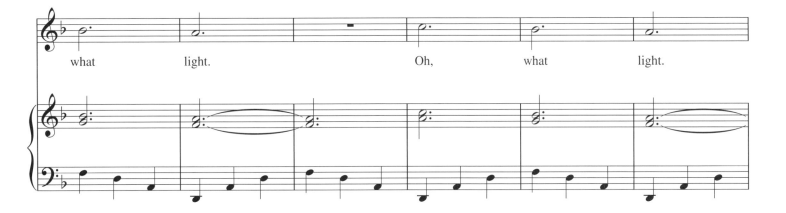

what   light.   Oh,   what   light.

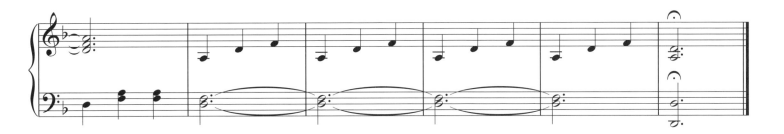

I AM A SEED

Words and Music by MARK WALDROP
and MIKE DODSON

Country Hoedown feel

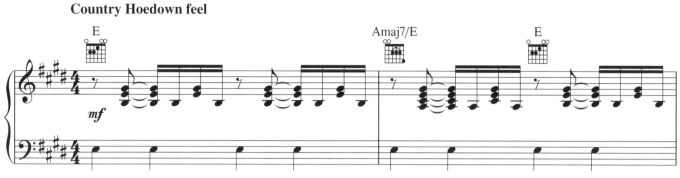

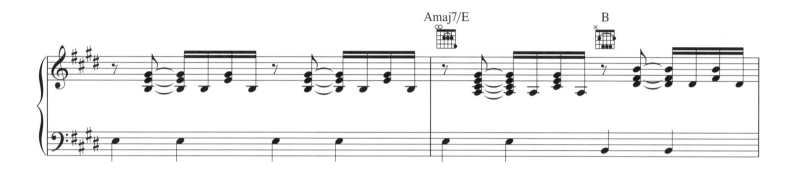

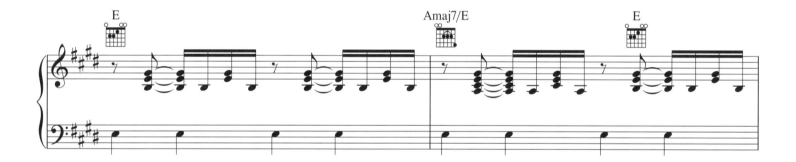

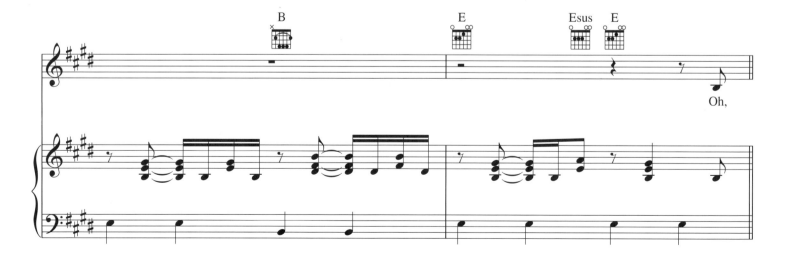

Oh,

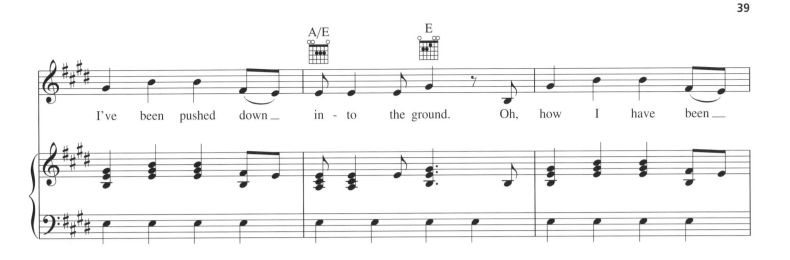

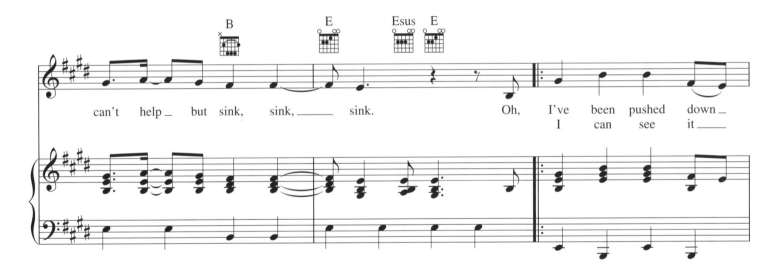

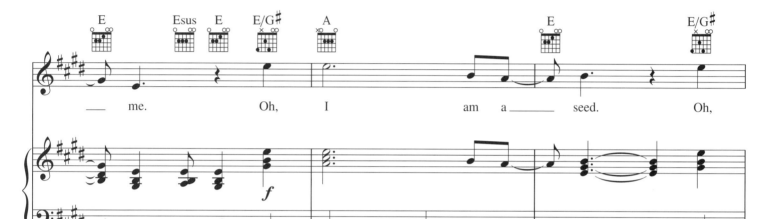

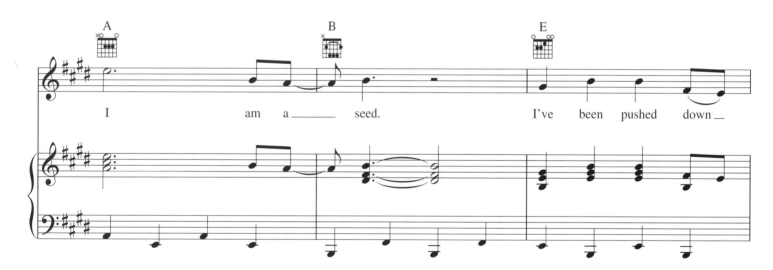

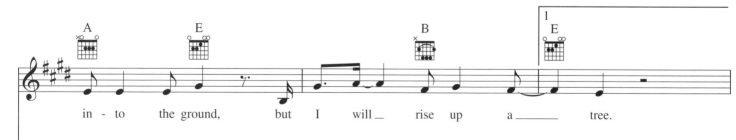

Oh, ____ tree. _____ Yeah!

I've been burned up __ in so man - y fires. From these ash - es

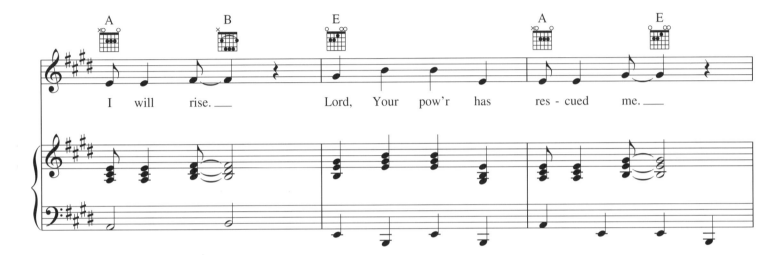

I will rise. __ Lord, Your pow'r has res - cued me. __

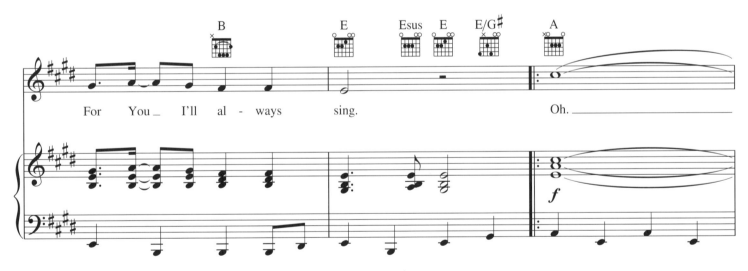

For You __ I'll al - ways sing. Oh. _____

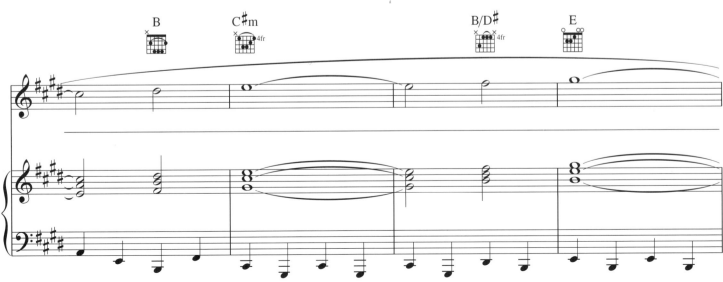

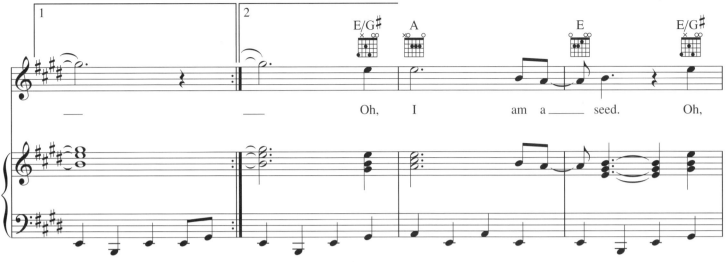

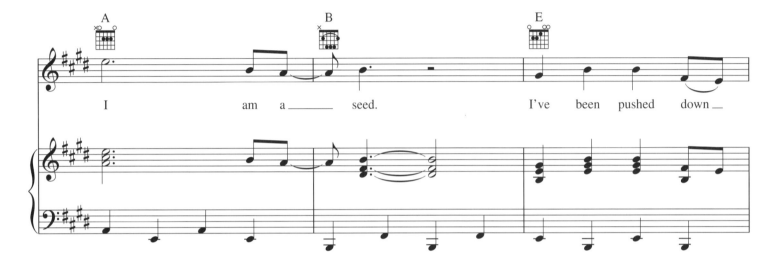

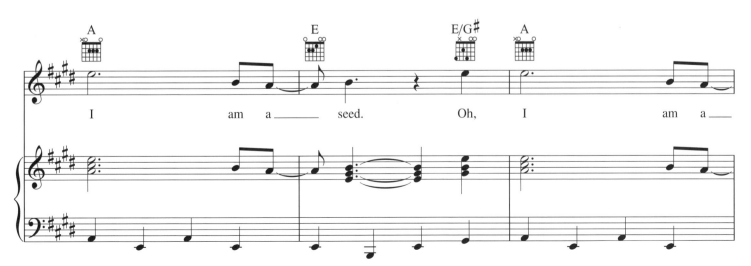

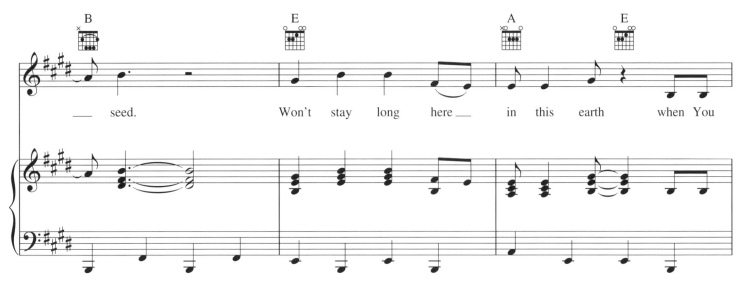

seed. Won't stay long here ___ in this earth when You

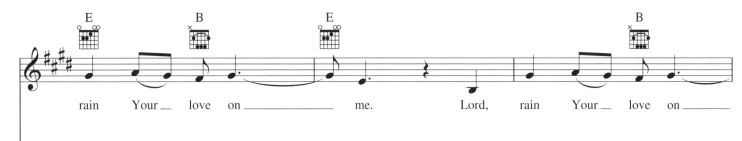

rain Your ___ love on _____ me. Lord, rain Your ___ love on _____

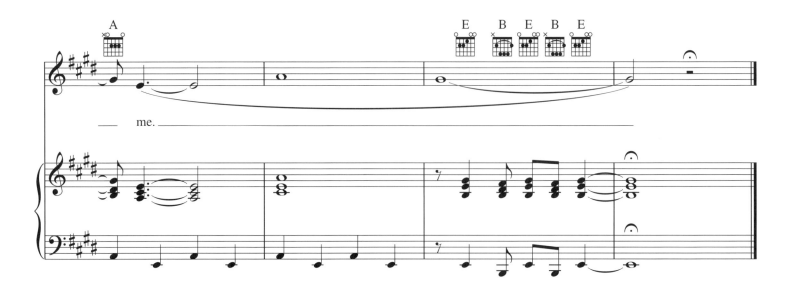

___ me. _____

AFTER ALL
(Holy)

Words and Music by DAVID CROWDER,
MARK WALDROP, MIKE DODSON
and MATT MAHER

In a strong 4

I can't com - pre - hend Your in - fi -

nite - ly beau - ti - ful and per - fect love. Oh, I've dreamed

dreams of maj - es - ty as bril - liant as a bil - lion

* Recorded a half step lower.

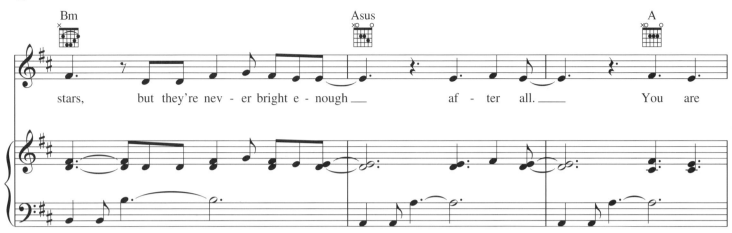

stars, but they're nev - er bright e - nough ___ af - ter all. ___ You are

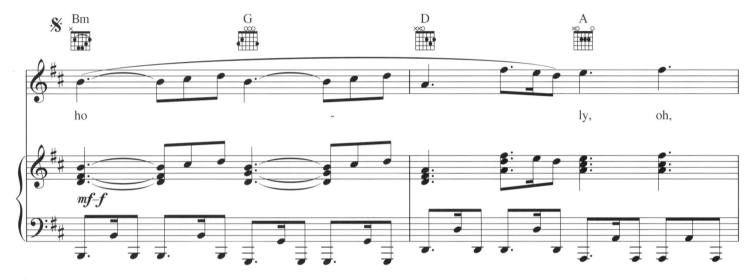

ho - ly, oh,

ho - ly, oh, ___

ho - ly, oh, ho -

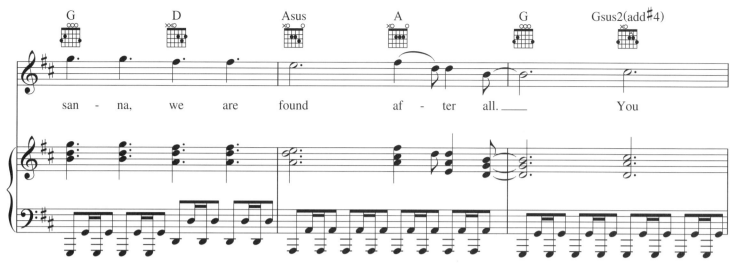

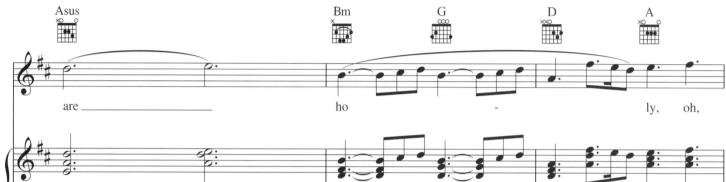

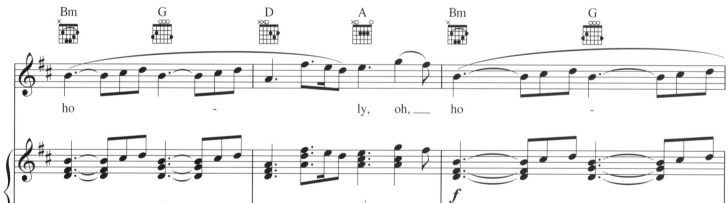

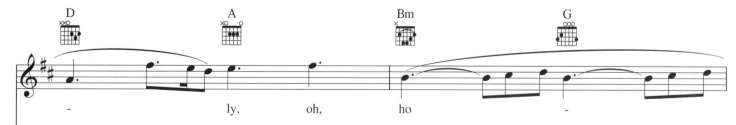

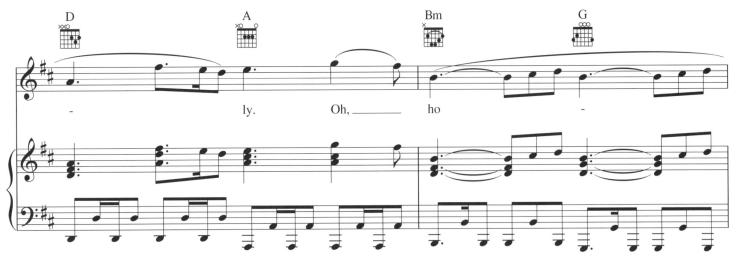

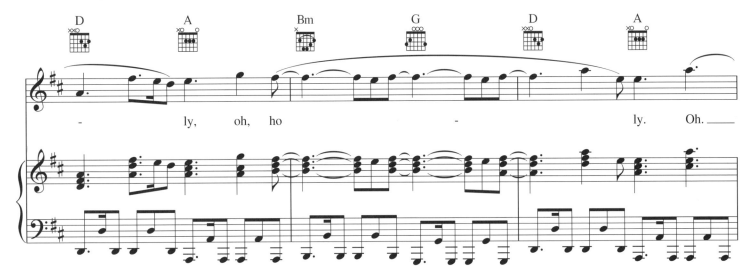

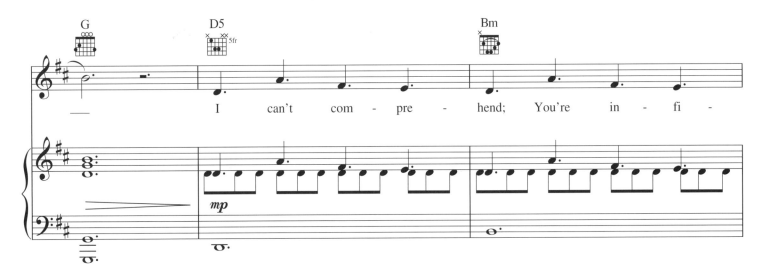

OH, GREAT LOVE OF GOD

Words and Music by DAVID CROWDER,
MARK WALDROP and MATT MAHER

Steady Rock beat

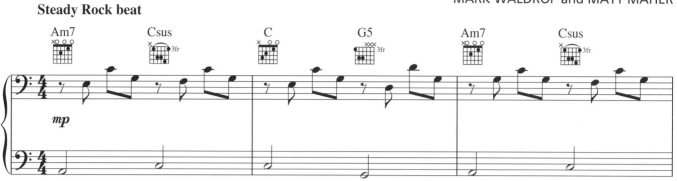

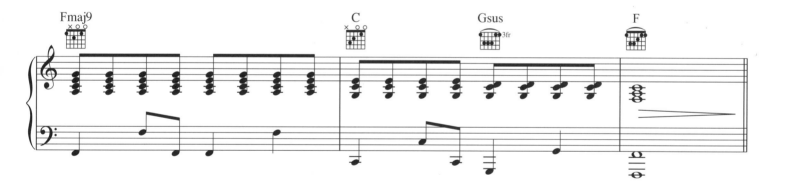

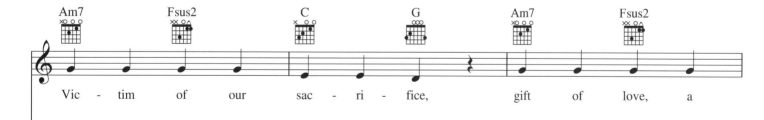

Vic-tim of our sac-ri-fice, gift of love, a

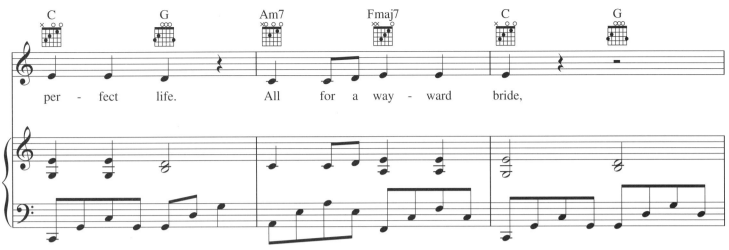

per - fect life. All for a way - ward bride,

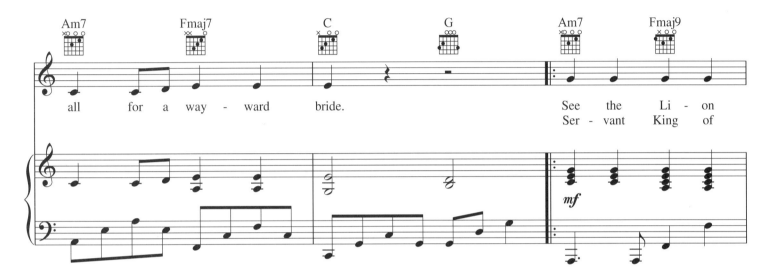

all for a way - ward bride. See the Li - on
Ser - vant King of

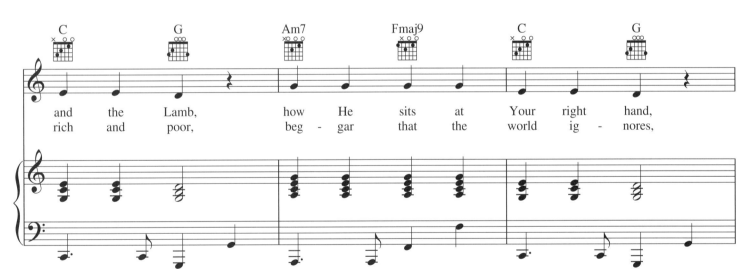

and the Lamb, how He sits at Your right hand,
rich and poor, beg - gar that the Your world ig - nores,

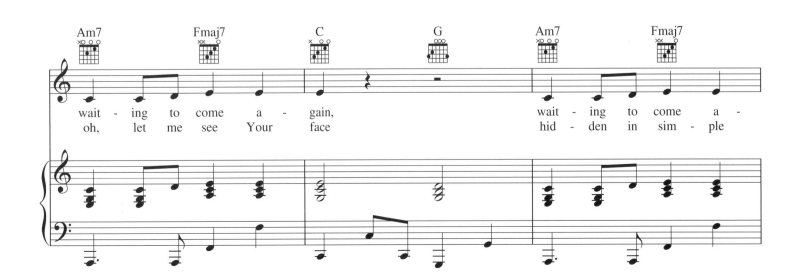

wait - ing to come a - gain,
oh, let me see Your face

wait - ing to come a -
hid - den in sim - ple

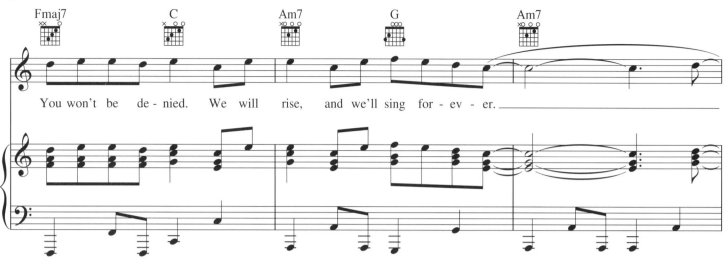

You won't be de - nied. We will rise, and we'll sing for - ev - er. _____

____ This is not a song; this is a re - viv - al, _____ a re -

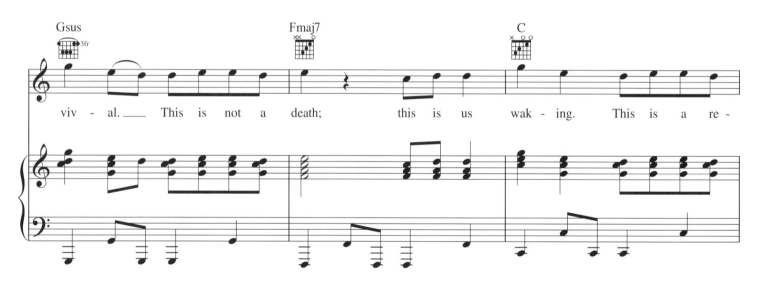

viv - al. ___ This is not a death; this is us wak - ing. This is a re -

turn back to life, oh, Your life, all I'm liv - ing for. Your life in my life, oh, it's

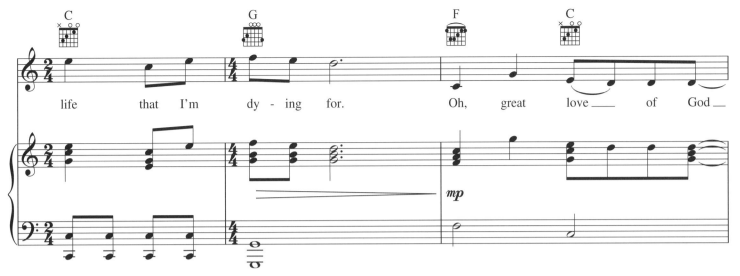

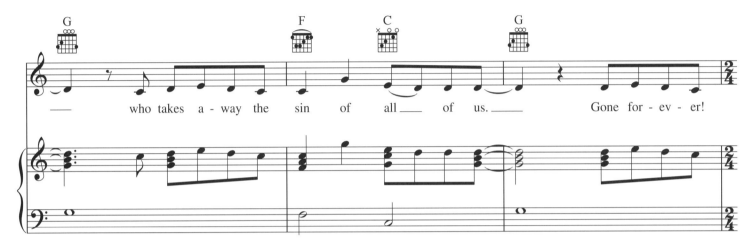

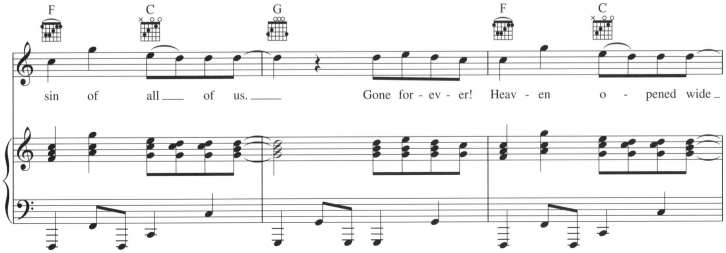

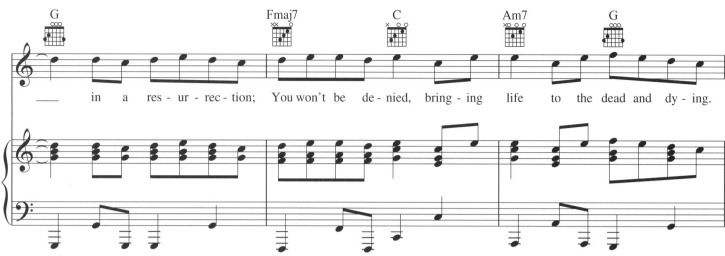

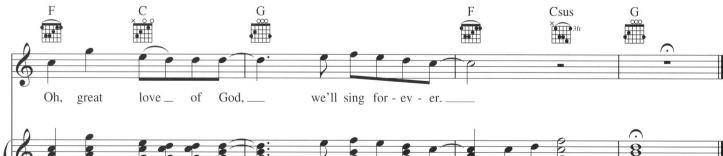

OUR COMMUNION

Words and Music by DAVID CROWDER,
JACK PARKER and MATT MAHER

Gently

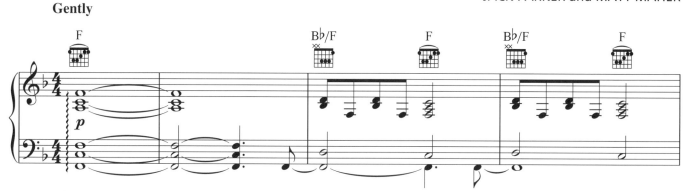

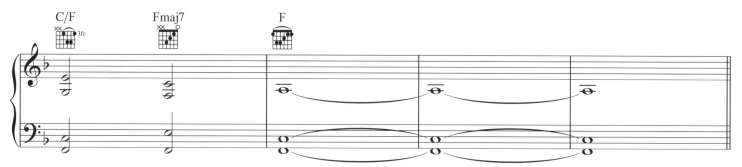

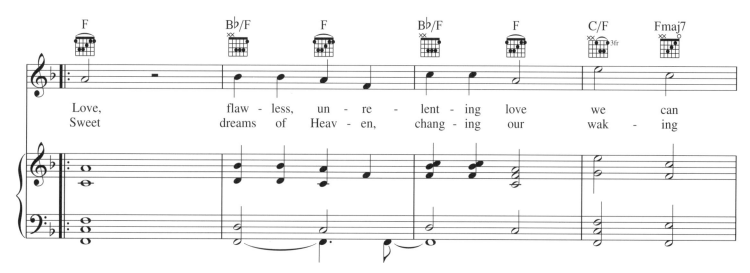

Love, flaw - less, un - re - lent - ing love we can
Sweet dreams of Heav - en, chang - ing our wak - ing

Play 1st time only

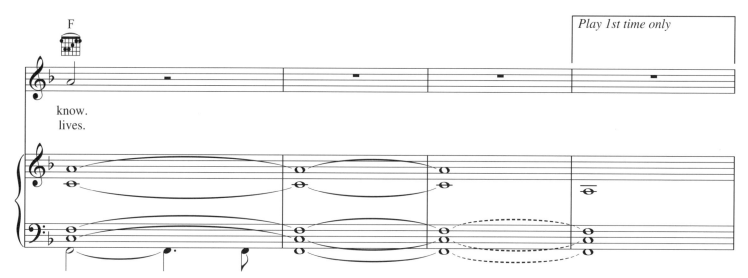

know.
lives.

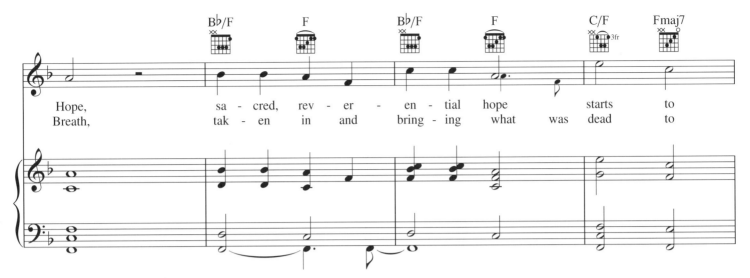

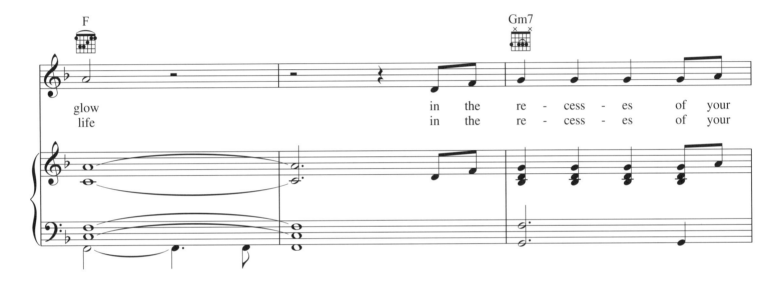

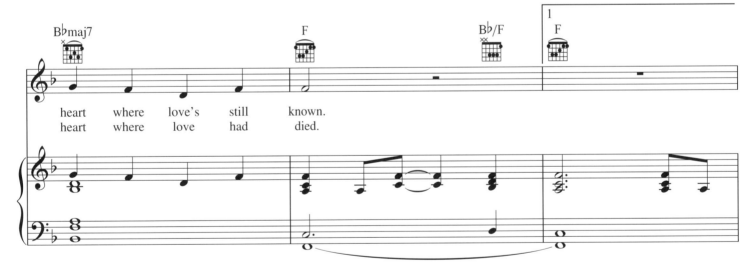

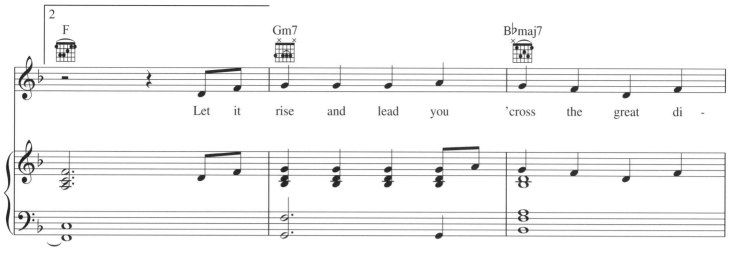

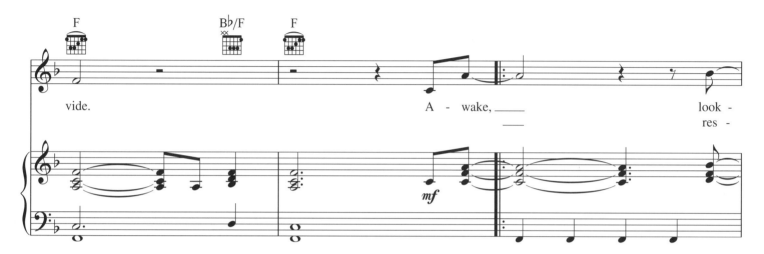

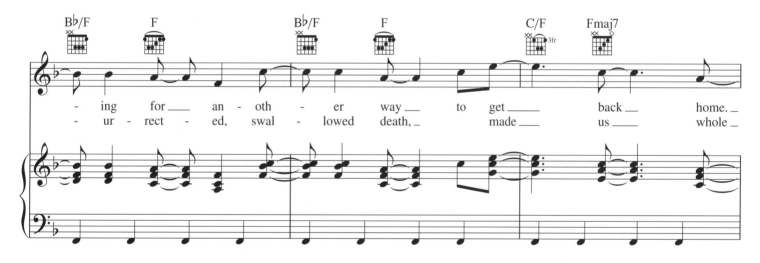

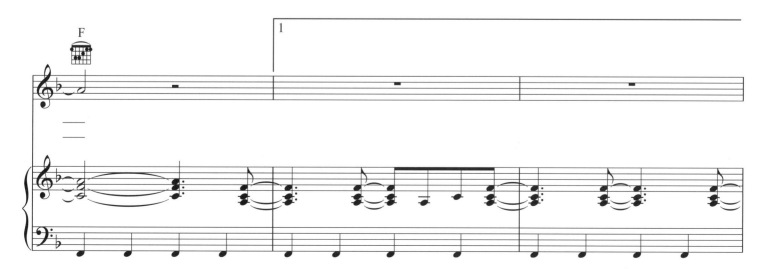

Life, ___ in the re - cess - es ___ of your heart ___

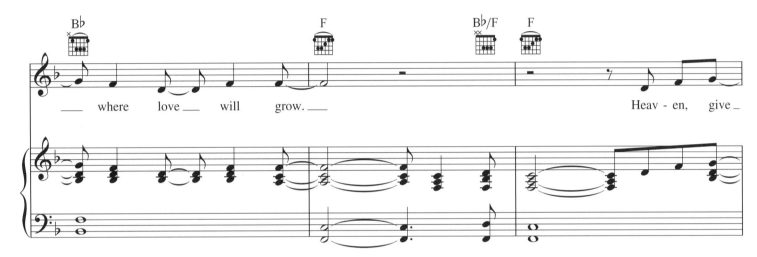

___ where love ___ will grow. ___ Heav - en, give ___

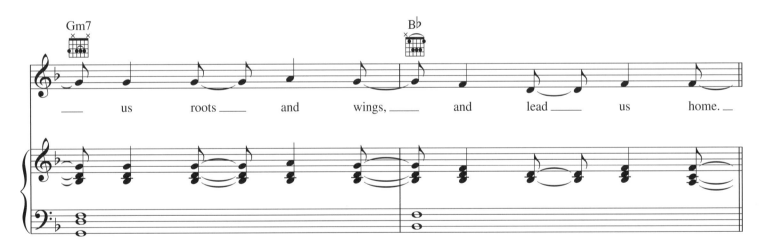

___ us roots ___ and wings, ___ and lead ___ us home. ___

Brightly

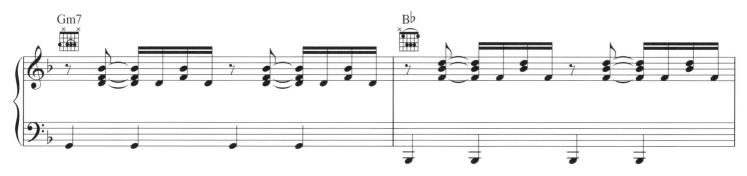

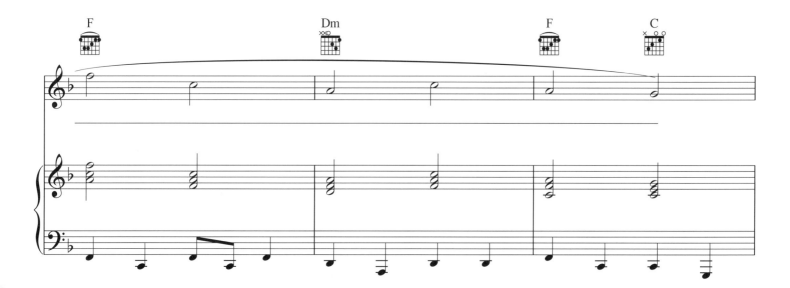

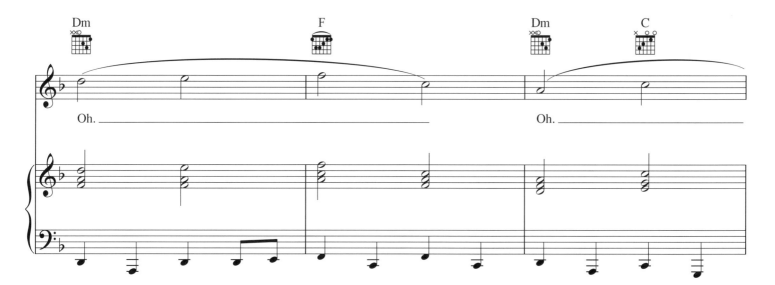

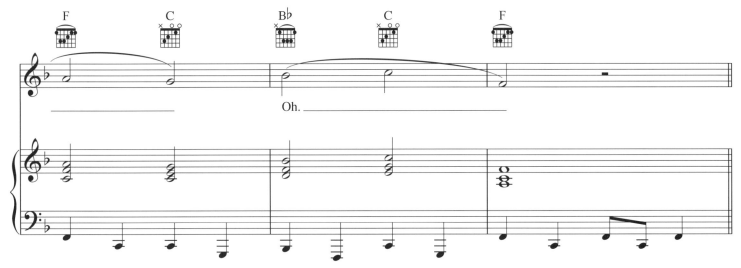

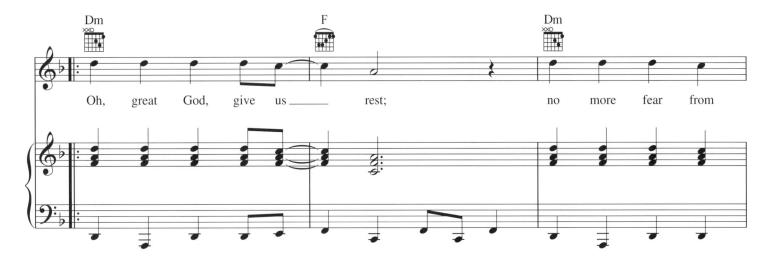

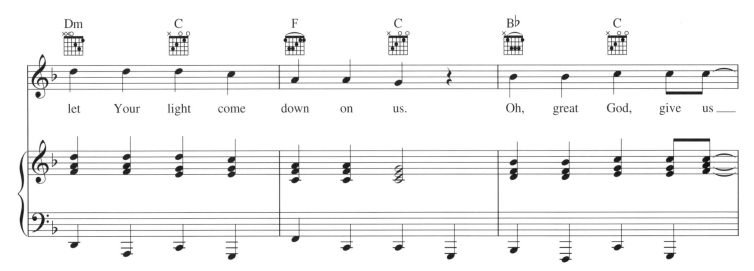

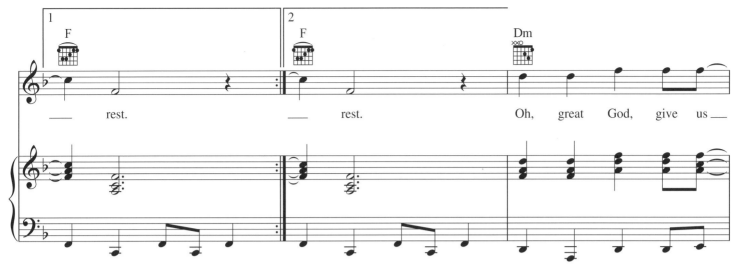

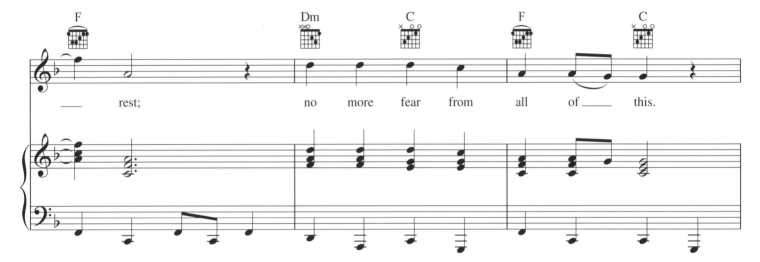

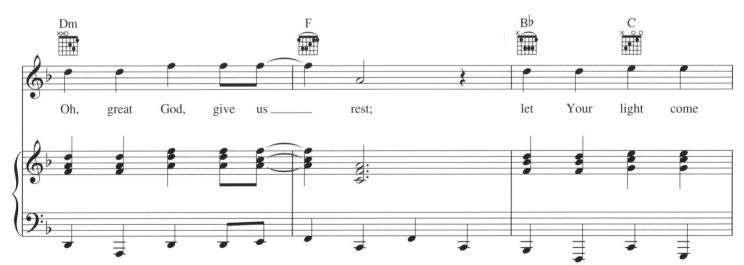

SOMETIMES

Words and Music by
DAVID CROWDER

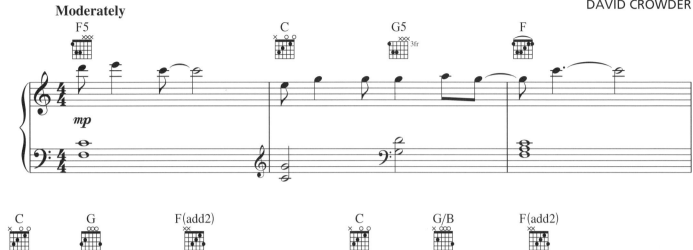

Some-times ____ ev-'ry one of us feels ____ like we'll

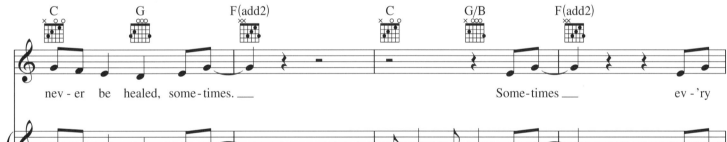

nev-er be healed, some-times. ____ Some-times ____ ev-'ry

one of us aches ____ like we'll nev-er be saved, some-times. ____

And when you've giv - en up, let your heal - ing come __ 'til you're

ris - ing up, let Your heal - ing come. __ It's Your love that we a - dore. It's like a

sea with - out a shore. We're lost ___ in You, __ we're lost ___ in You. __ It's Your

love that we a - dore. It's like a sea with - out a shore. We're lost ___ in You, we're lost __

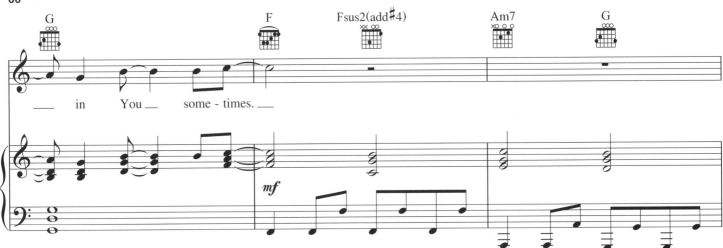

in You some - times.

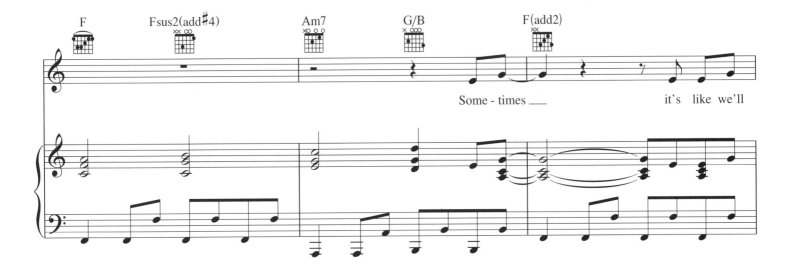

Some - times it's like we'll

nev - er a - tone for all the love we've known. Some - times,

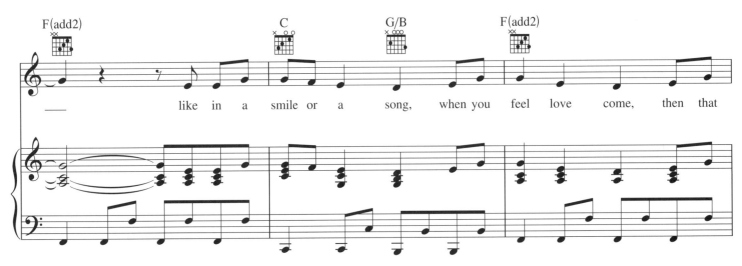

like in a smile or a song, when you feel love come, then that

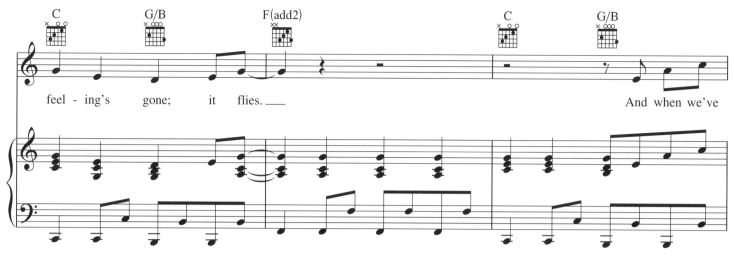

feel - ing's gone; it flies. ____ And when we've

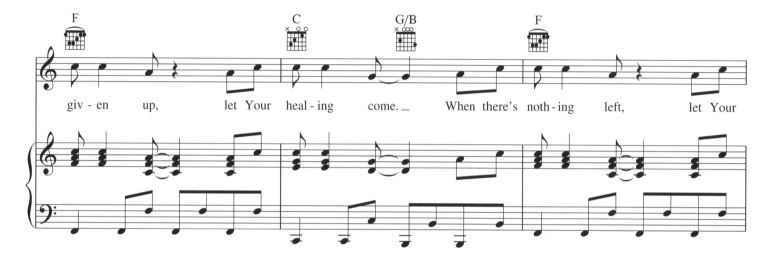

giv - en up, let Your heal - ing come. ____ When there's noth - ing left, let Your

heal - ing come. ____ 'Til we're ris - ing up, let Your heal - ing come. ____ Where You

go, ____ we will fol - low. ____ Where You go, ____ we will fol - low, ____

oh. _____ It's Your love that we a-dore. It's like a sea with-out a shore. We're lost _____

_____ in You, _____ we're lost _____ in You. _ And it's Your love that we a-dore. It's like a

sea with-out a shore. We're lost _____ in You, we're lost _____ in You. _ And it's Your

love that we a-dore. It's like a sea with-out a shore. We're lost _____ in You, we're lost _____

grace._____ Let's risk the o - cean;_____ there's on - ly grace._____ Let's risk the o -

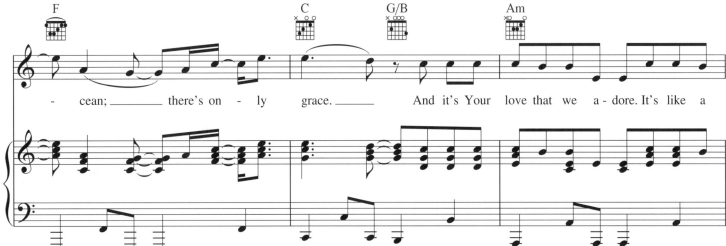

- cean;_____ there's on - ly grace._____ And it's Your love that we a - dore. It's like a

sea with-out a shore. We're lost_____ in You,_ we're lost_____ in You._ And it's Your

love that we a - dore. It's like a sea with-out a shore. We're lost_____ in You, we're lost_

A RETURN

Words and Music by DAVID CROWDER
and MARK WALDROP

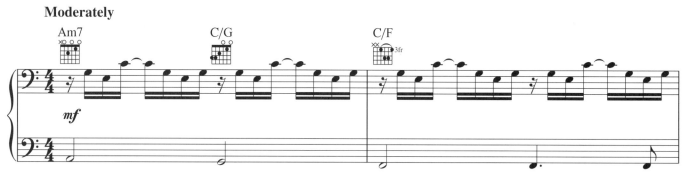

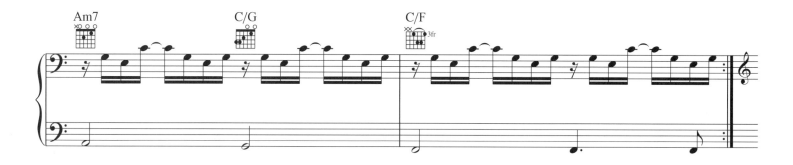

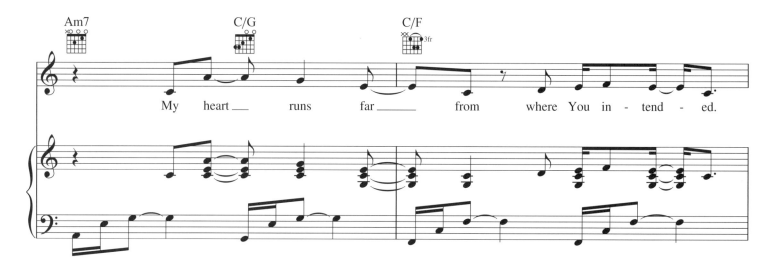

My heart ___ runs far ___ from where You in - tend - ed.

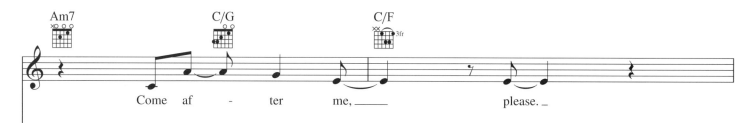

Come af - ter me, ___ please. ___

My heart ___ runs far _____ from where You ___ in-tend - ed.

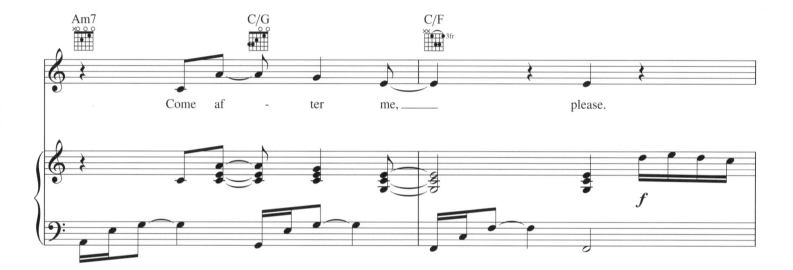

Come af - ter me, _____ please.

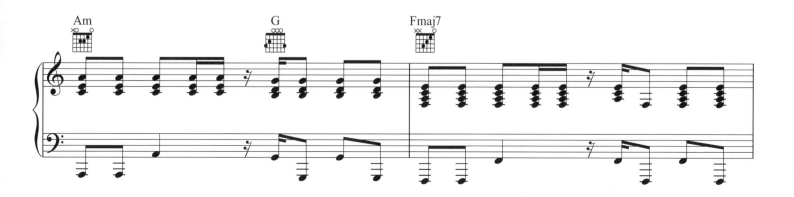

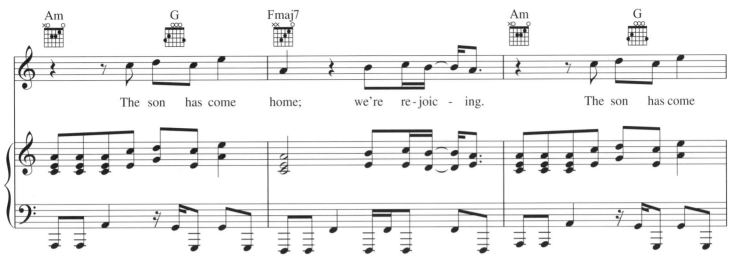

The son has come home; we're re-joic - ing. The son has come

home; re - joice, my __ soul. __ The son has come

home; we're re-joic - ing. The son has come

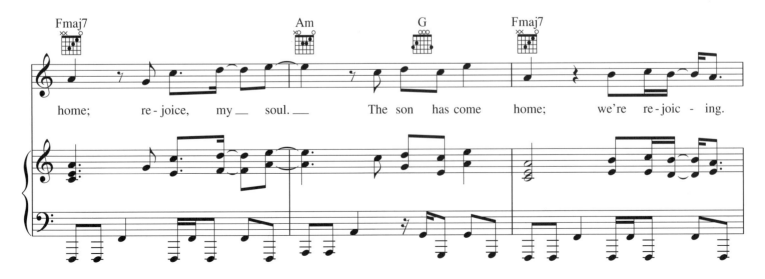

home; re - joice, my __ soul. __ The son has come home; we're re-joic - ing.

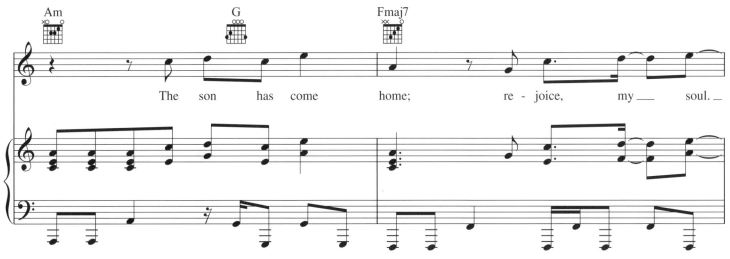

The son has come home; re - joice, my ___ soul. ___

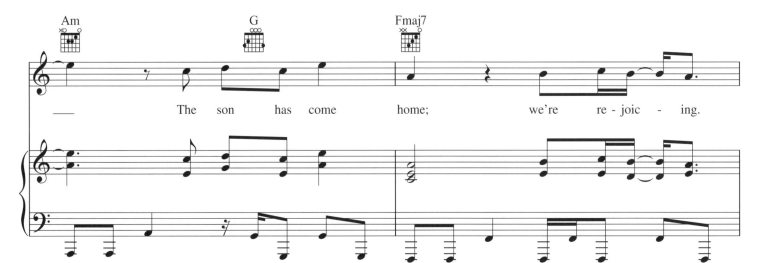

___ The son has come home; we're re - joic - ing.

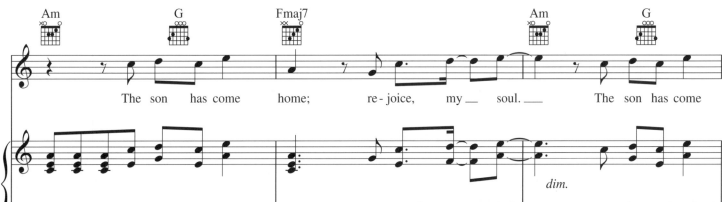

The son has come home; re - joice, my ___ soul. ___ The son has come

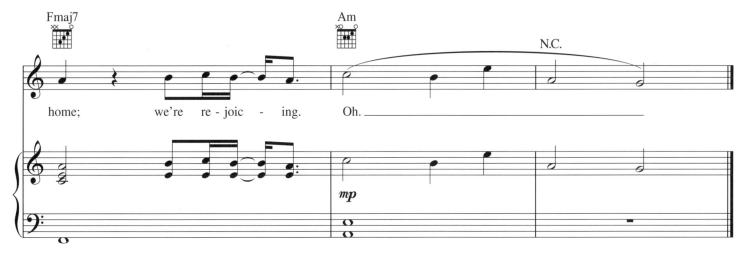

home; we're re - joic - ing. Oh. ___

LEANING ON THE EVERLASTING ARMS/ 'TIS SO SWEET TO TRUST IN JESUS

Traditional
Arranged by DAVID CROWDER

Bluegrass feel

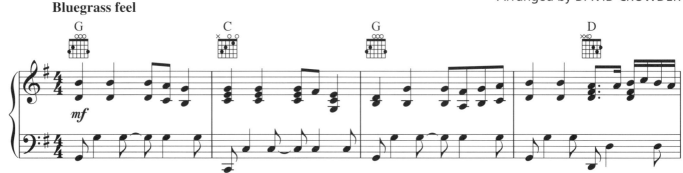

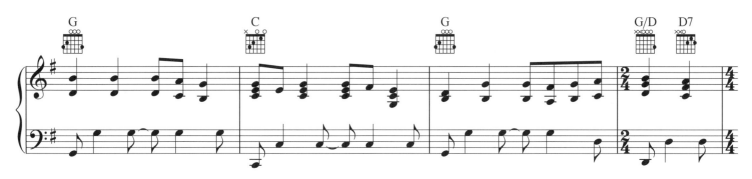

What a fel-low-ship, what a joy di-vine,
O how sweet to walk in the pil-grim way,

(D.S.) *Instrumental*

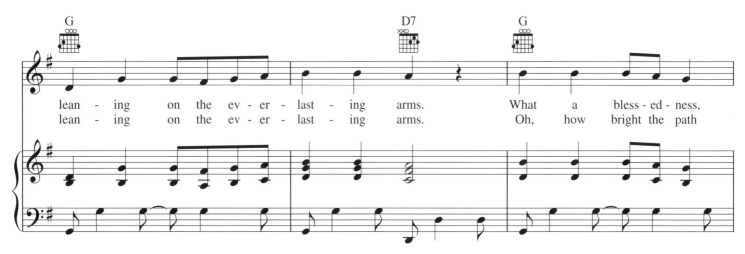

lean - ing on the ev-er - last - ing arms. What a bless-ed - ness,
lean - ing on the ev-er - last - ing arms. Oh, how bright the path

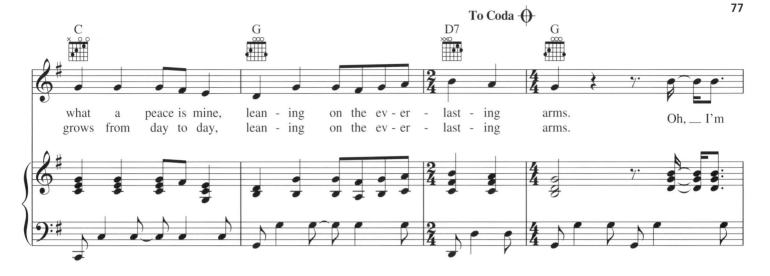

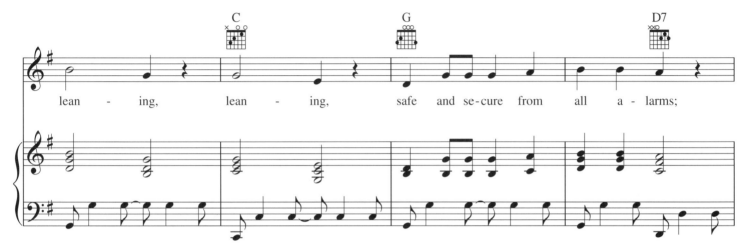

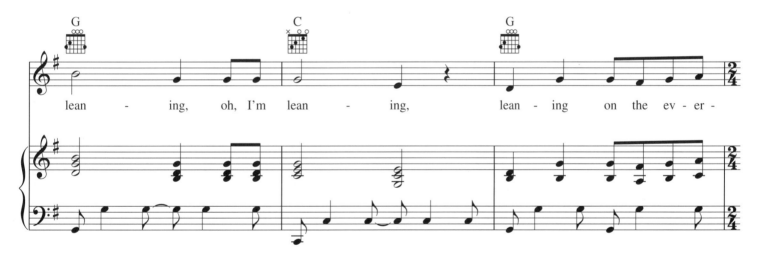

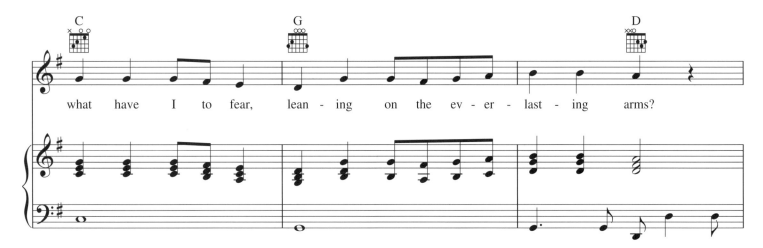

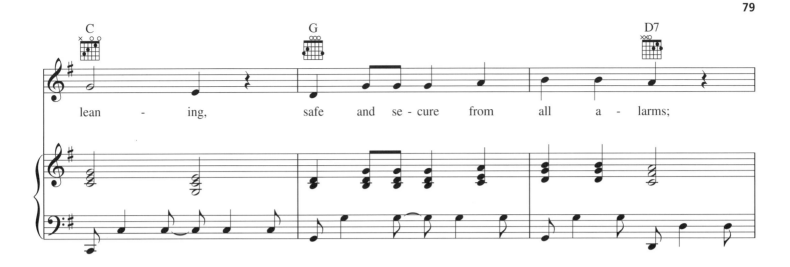

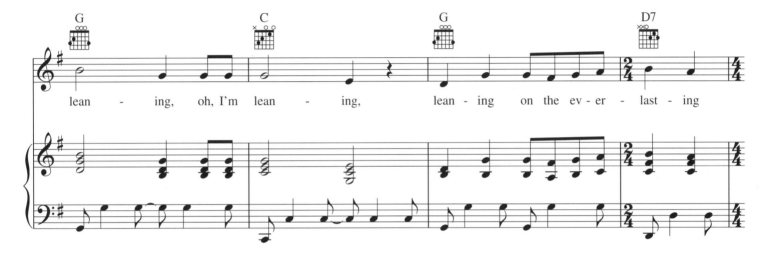

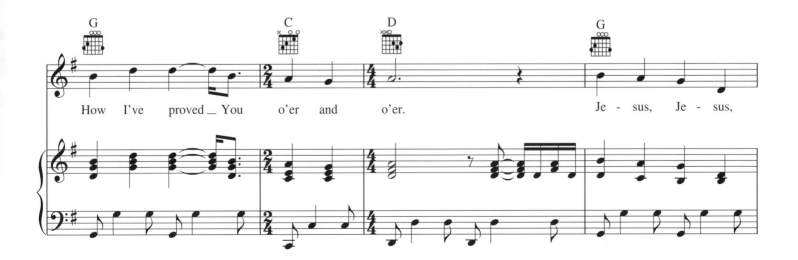

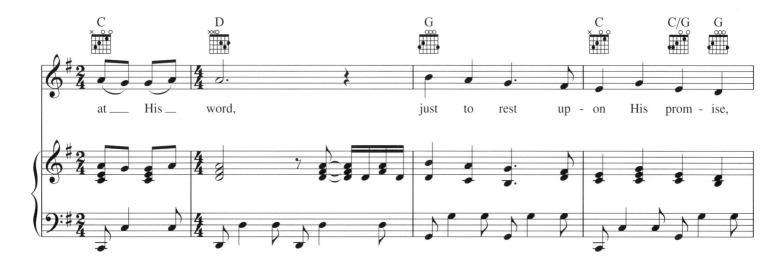

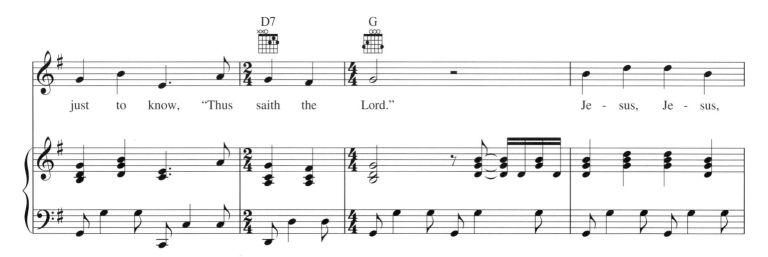

how I trust Him. How I've proved ___ Him o'er ___ and ___

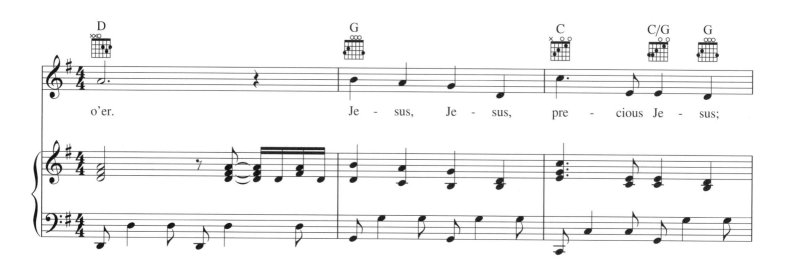

o'er. Je - sus, Je - sus, pre - cious Je - sus;

oh, for grace to trust Him more. Oh, for grace to

trust Him more. Oh, for grace to trust Him more.

JESUS, LEAD ME TO YOUR HEALING WATERS

Words and Music by DAVID CROWDER,
MARK WALDROP, MIKE DODSON,
MIKE HOGAN and JACK PARKER

Je - sus, _____ lead ___ me to Your heal - ing wa-

- ters. _____ Take ___ me down ___

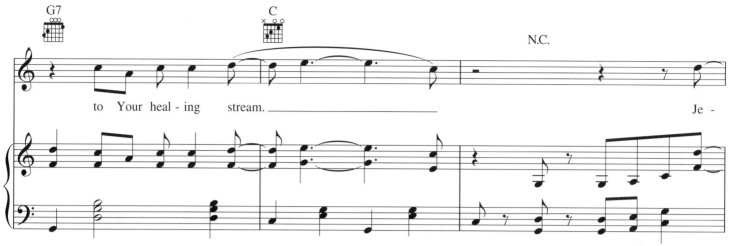

to Your heal - ing stream. _____ Je -

- sus, _____ lead _____ me to Your heal - ing wa - ters. _____

Take ___ me down ___ and wash _____ me clean. ___

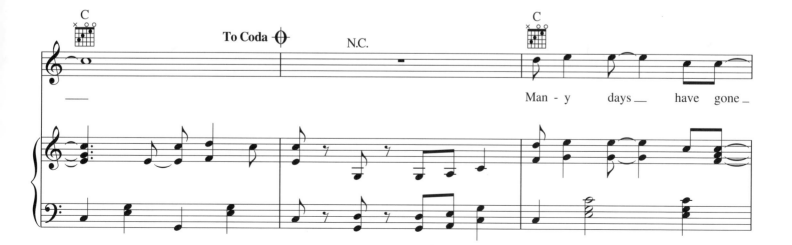

Man - y days ___ have gone ___

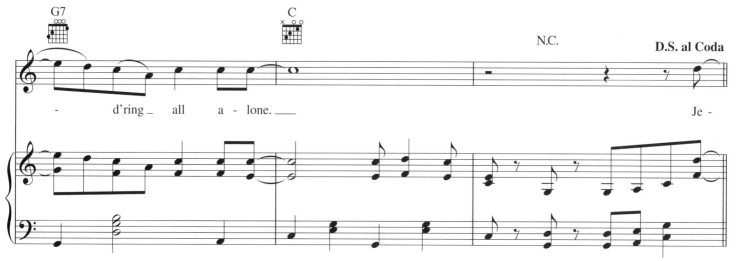

d'ring __ all a - lone. ____ Je -

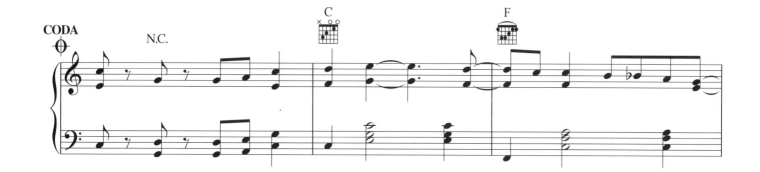

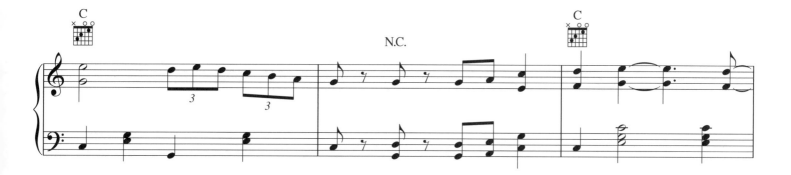

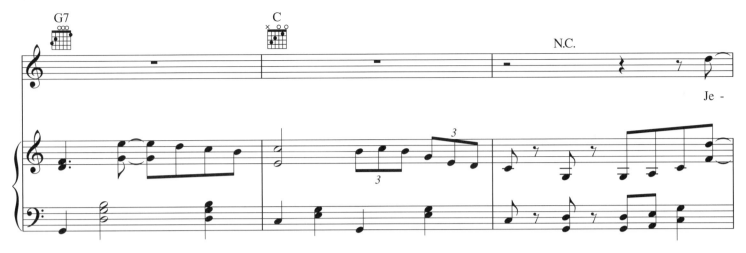

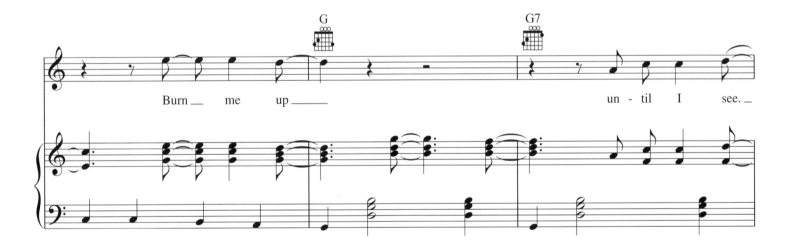

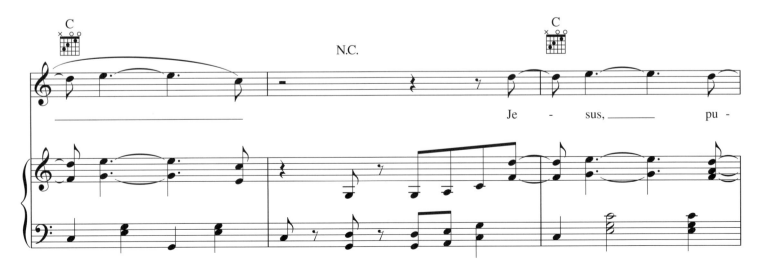

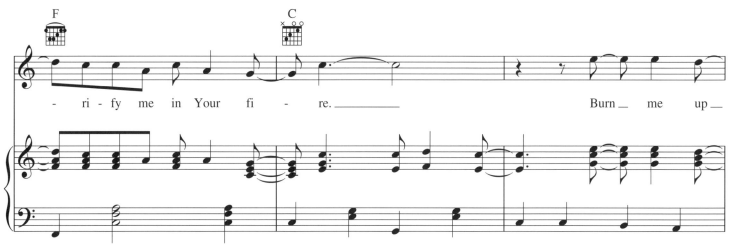

-ri - fy me in Your fi - re. _____ Burn ___ me up ___

___ un - til I _____ be - lieve. ___

Man - y days ___ have gone, ___ yet still I loved ___

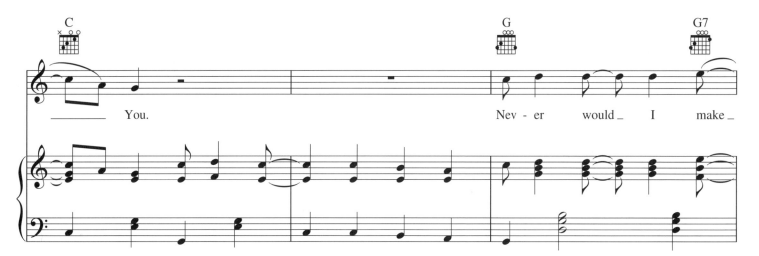

_____ You.   Nev - er would ___ I make ___

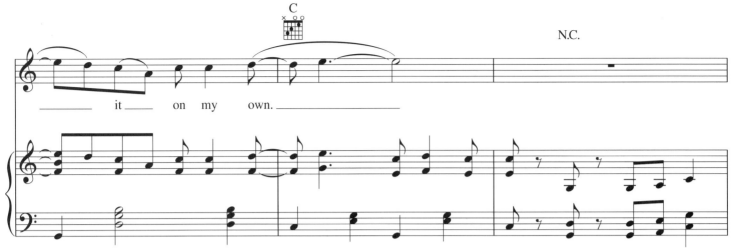

it __ on my own. _____

This life here _____ and now _____ is where I need ___ You,

and then up there ___ is when _____ I'm ___ fi - n'lly home. _

___ Je - sus, _____ oh, __

and set ___ me free. ___   Oh, take ___ me up ___

___   and set ___ me free. ___

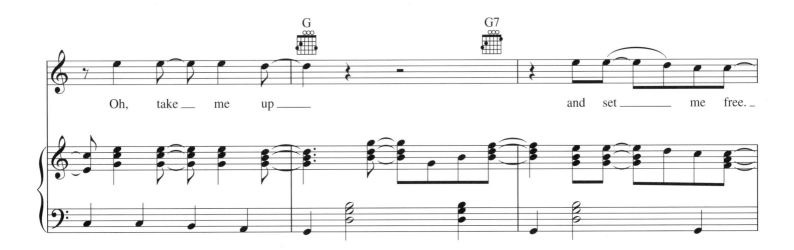

Oh, take ___ me up ___   and set ___ me free. ___

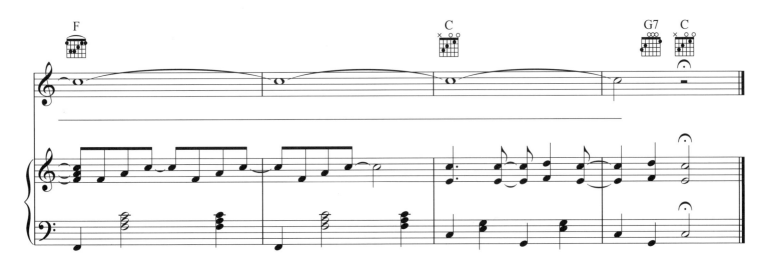

BECAUSE HE LIVES

Words by WILLIAM J. and GLORIA GAITHER
Music by WILLIAM J. GAITHER

Moderately slow

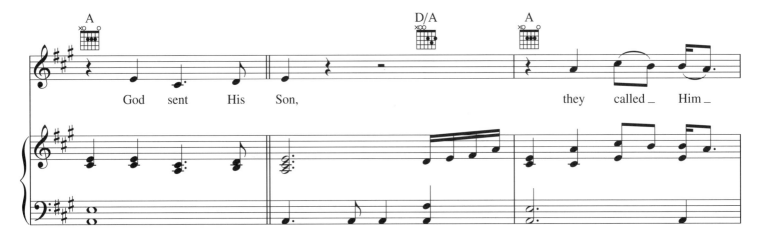

God sent His Son, they called _ Him _

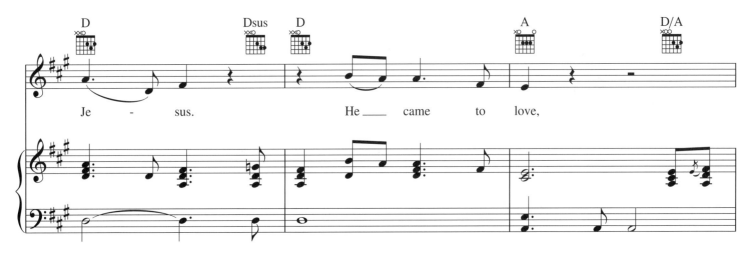

Je - sus. He _ came to love,

heal _ and for - give.

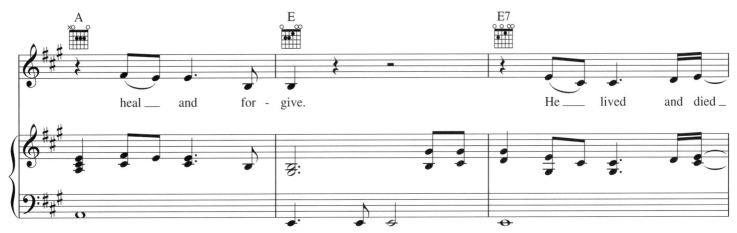

He _ lived and died _

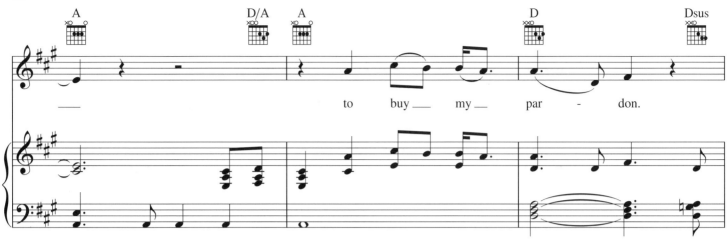

to buy ___ my ___ par - don.

An emp - ty ___ grave is there _____ to ___ prove my Sav - ior ___

gradual cresc.

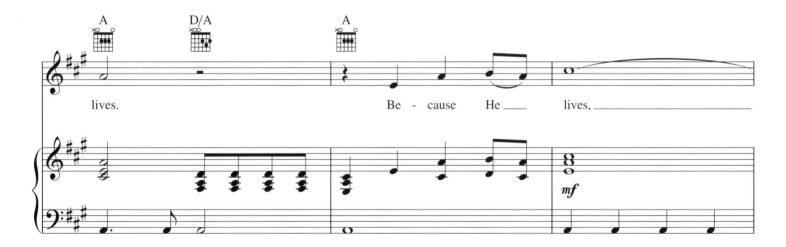

lives.   Be - cause He ___ lives, _____

mf

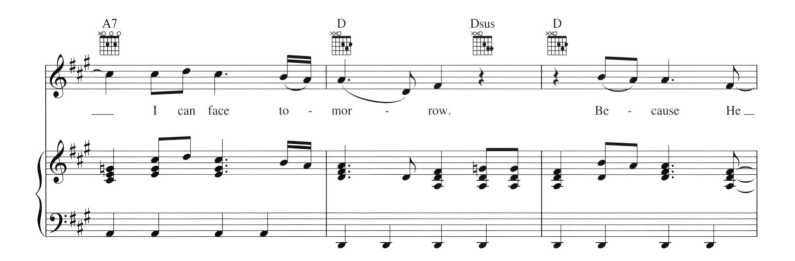

___ I can face to - mor - row.   Be - cause He ___

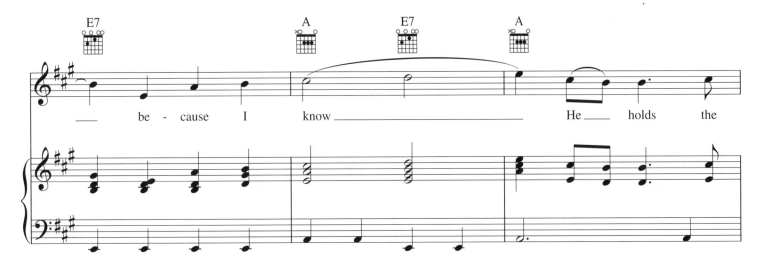

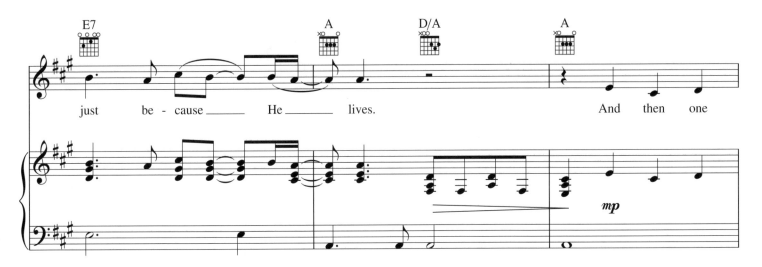

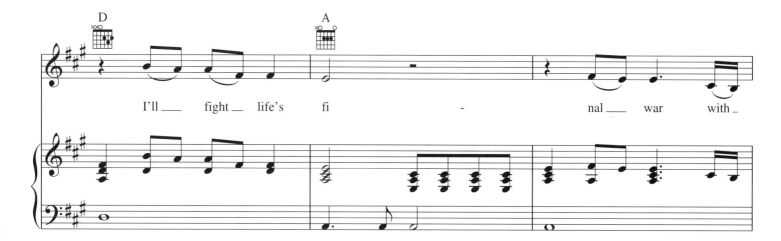

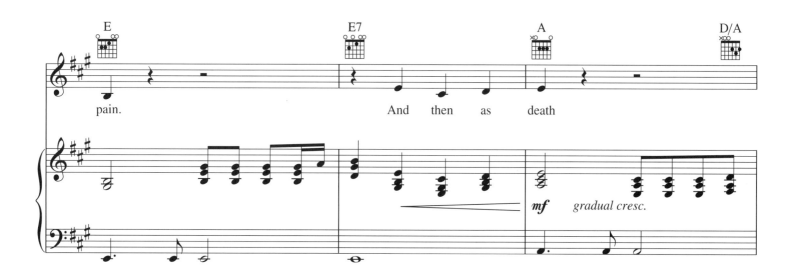

lights of glo - ry and I'll know __ He __ lives. __

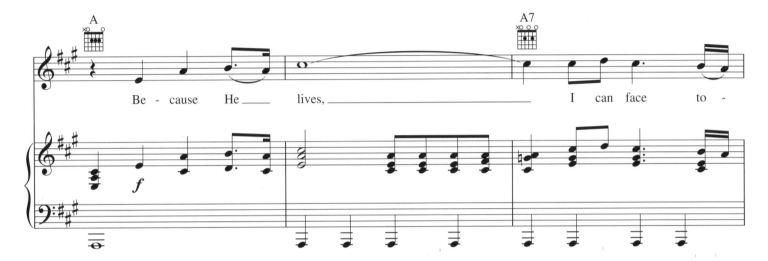

Be - cause He __ lives, _____ I can face to -

mor - row. Be - cause __ He lives,

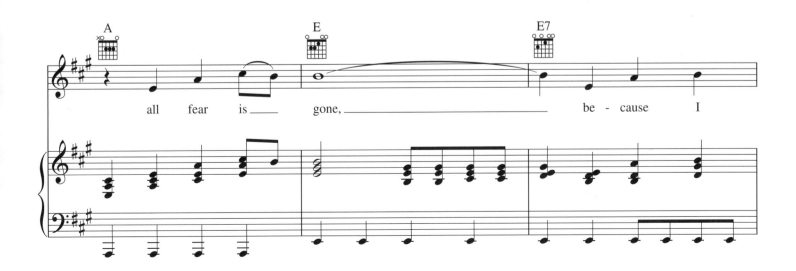

all fear is __ gone, _____ be - cause I

know _____ He __ holds the fu - ture,

and life is __ worth the liv - ing just be - cause __ He __

__ lives. And life is __ worth the liv - ing

just be - cause __ He __ lives. _____